T0149253

They Say You Are Saved

BUT, WHAT IF THEY ARE WRONG?

MARTY VANDERZANDEN

WESTBOW
PRESS®
A DIVISION OF THOMAS NELSON
& ZONDERVAN

Scripture taken from the Holy Bible, NEW INTERNATIONAL
VERSION®. Copyright © 1973, 1978, 1984 by Biblica, Inc.
All rights reserved worldwide. Used by permission. NEW
INTERNATIONAL VERSION® and NIV® are registered trademarks
of Biblica, Inc. Use of either trademark for the offering of goods or
services requires the prior written consent of Biblica US, Inc.

WestBow Press books may be ordered through booksellers or by contacting:

WestBow Press
A Division of Thomas Nelson & Zondervan
1663 Liberty Drive
Bloomington, IN 47403
www.westbowpress.com
1 (866) 928-1240

Because of the dynamic nature of the Internet, any web addresses or
links contained in this book may have changed since publication and
may no longer be valid. The views expressed in this work are solely those
of the author and do not necessarily reflect the views of the publisher,
and the publisher hereby disclaims any responsibility for them.

Any people depicted in stock imagery provided by Thinkstock are models,
and such images are being used for illustrative purposes only.
Certain stock imagery © Thinkstock.

ISBN: 978-1-5127-2513-1 (sc)
ISBN: 978-1-5127-2514-8 (e)

Library of Congress Control Number: 2015921388

Print information available on the last page.

WestBow Press rev. date: 2/10/2016

CONTENTS

ACKNOWLEDGMENTS

Writing this book has been an amazing journey, and I have many people to thank.

First of all, I thank God. This book is His message, and He inspired me to write it. To God be the glory!

Next, I thank my dear wife, Connie, who by God's grace has learned how to unconditionally love me. She inspires me and listens to me so patiently. She reminds me of Proverbs 31:10, "A wife of noble character who can find? She is worth far more than rubies." Thank you, Connie, for your patience, love, and kindness. Mostly, I thank you for your prayers. There is nothing like the prayers of a loving wife. I have heard it said that behind every good husband is a great wife. Because of you, I now understand the meaning of this.

I thank my children, for I have learned much from them. Andrea, from you I have learned the meaning of unconditional love, acceptance, and patience. Megan, from you I have learned that when God strengthens me and I walk in His way, I can do anything. Jake, from you I have learned a new level of peace, how to be more content in life, and how to enjoy the simple pleasures of God.

Last, I thank the many people God has placed in my path who have supported me in prayer, read various drafts of this book, and given me honest feedback. May God bless you and keep you. May He be the center of your life and the desire of your heart.

PREFACE

The thought of eternal life with Jesus in heaven has never been a topic I could fully comprehend. My simple mind just doesn't seem to have what it takes to understand what life will be like in heaven. I have heard many people talking about how wonderful heaven will be; they tell me we will be with God all the time and worship Him. There will be no more pain or suffering or sin. They say life will be awesome and we will get to sing with the choir of heaven. Living in heaven is very appealing to me. It is like home. I miss being home in heaven and I can't wait to get there.

I don't hear too many people willing to talk about hell. Those who are willing, describe it as a dark place where Satan and his followers will be sent, a place devoid of peace or joy. In hell, there is constant pain, intense heat, eternal suffering, and worst of all, you would not be in the presence of God. It sounds terrible.

All my life, I was told that to avoid spending eternity in hell, all I had to do was accept Jesus as my Lord and Savior and say a prayer. Then I need no longer worry about going to hell. It was that simple. Say the prayer, God will bless you, life will be great, and you will be guaranteed a place in heaven.

I was in fourth grade when I said the prayer for the first time. I thought to myself, *Who wants to spend eternity in hell, anyway? If all I have to do is say a prayer, then why not say the prayer and get it over with? After that, my eternity in heaven will be certain. I won't have to worry about going to hell, because I said the prayer.* Or so I thought.

My life continued. I considered myself a Christian because I had said the prayer, believed in God who created the earth, and sometimes attended church. But if you were to examine the details of my life, you would have found very little evidence either that I was a Christian or that I was making any attempt to follow Jesus and His teachings.

I was living for myself. Jesus was not a priority in my life. I had said the prayer, I was a nice guy, I helped people, I gave some money away, and I had many friends, so I figured I would be going to heaven when I died. I thought, *If this is how it works, then I'll go for it and live out the American dream. I'll work hard, make money, and do what I want.* I thought God would be with me to help me achieve my goals and my desires because He loved me and wanted the best for me. When life wasn't going my way, I thought God would be there to change things and make them better for me. My existence was so much about me, my way, and my own desire. I was not seeking God or trying to live His way.

This lifestyle had a devastating impact on my life and on the lives of others. I got married twice and divorced twice. I became an alcoholic and used drugs. I thought premarital sex was acceptable, got a woman pregnant, and convinced her to abort the child. My life was a mess.

During the last five years of my drinking days, I was in a formal Bible study. I'm not sure why I did this; maybe it was because I enjoyed the Monday evenings after Bible study. I'd go out, have some beers, smoke cigars, look at women, and act in ways that were most certainly detestable to God.

If you were to ask me at that time whether I was a Christian, I would have said yes. If you had asked me whether I knew where I would spend eternity, I would have said heaven, because I had said the prayer one day and the deal was done. I had been told Jesus died for all my sins to be forgiven, so no matter what I did after I had said the prayer, I never again had to worry about going to hell.

Down deep in my heart, I knew this was not right—I knew there was more. I had been studying the Bible but hadn't yet found the verse that said all I had to do was say a prayer and then I was going to heaven. My studying the Bible for those five years now seems more like an intellectual experience than a spiritual, heart-filled one. Nonetheless, I was studying God's Word, and it was somehow getting into my heart.

After the end of one Bible study, I sat in the church sanctuary alone. My life as I knew it was crashing down all around me. I was going through my second divorce and I had lost my job, stopped drinking, and entered an alcohol treatment program. I had never felt so alone. All of a sudden, God decided to pay me a special visit. He brought His presence to me in a way that was initially frightening. But when I finally settled down, I realized God was not there to hurt me. He said, "You have been studying my Word for the past five years." He asked me if I believed what I was reading in the Bible.

I knew this was a critical point in my life. There I was, in the presence of God, and He was speaking to me and asking me a very direct question. I told Him, yes, I did believe what was in the Bible. He then asked, "When are you going to start living your life as if you believe?"

That question broke my heart. I wept in that church pew for a long time, crying until I couldn't cry anymore. I told God I understood what He was asking of me and said I would need His help because I had no idea how to live a Christian life and follow His Son, Jesus Christ. I could sense God smile, and then the experience was over.

Over the next few months, some amazing things happened to me. People I didn't know came up to me in church and offered to pray for me. A gentleman told me about a mentorship program the church was running and invited me to join it. God was faithful in providing the help He promised me.

I started to pray and understand that prayer was more than just connecting with God when I needed something from Him; I found that prayer was a time I could connect with God just to be with Him. I enjoyed being with God— and you know what? He enjoys being with me. I felt loved, cared for, and for the first time in my life, I felt whole.

I allowed God free reign in my heart, and He transformed me. This process of intense transformation took about three years. The old Marty listened to rock and roll, the louder the better, but during this period, the only music I could tolerate was soft piano music. Sex and violence usually made for a great movie-watching experience for the old Marty, but during this transformation period, the only movies I could watch were the sappiest love stories, and I would sob during them.

At this time, I learned how to develop a relationship with Jesus Christ. I started learning about humility and what it was like to honor others above myself. God became more to me than an eternal safety net; He became my best friend. He and I have spent much time together. I share with Him the deepest desires of my heart, and He tells me He already knows them—He put them there.

Nobody had ever before told me or tried to teach me about having a deep, close, and personal relationship with Jesus. I'd heard people saying that we could have a relationship with Jesus, but nobody explained how to achieve that. People talked about their earthly relationships, but nobody was talking about their personal relationship with Jesus. It had all seemed so elusive to me.

And remember: the old Marty had no reason to follow Jesus; he had been told that his salvation was sealed. Also, he was searching out the American dream. He didn't think he needed a relationship with Jesus; he considered it optional. The old Marty saw Jesus as someone who would have told him to stop drinking or having fun.

After this three-year period of transformation, God started putting my life back together, one piece at a time, but this time, He was building it on a foundation of faith and an intimate relationship with Him. God introduced me to my best earthly friend, Connie. We met on an Internet dating site. She's a wonderful Christian woman. We got married and even now continue to grow in our faith together.

I started to develop an unquenchable thirst for God and His Word. I couldn't get enough of God. I wanted to talk to everyone about Him and what He had done for me. He was constantly on my mind. When I was not in church or reading the Bible, I was listening to sermons from churches all over the nation on CD's, the Internet and podcasts.

I started to meet with men who considered themselves Christians, but they reminded me of the old Marty. They had said the prayer, they were going to church, and they were nice guys, but if you asked them about their personal relationship with Jesus, they would not be able to describe it; instead, they would get uncomfortable and try to end the conversation. The more I looked around, the more I found people who seemed to have a casual relationship with Jesus. I prayed and asked God to help me understand the concept of saying a prayer and being saved, because it didn't feel right in my heart.

After several years of prayer, I received an interesting answer from God. He told me that He wanted me to write a book for Him. I kind of chuckled when He first said that, because I had never authored anything besides a college term paper, e-mail, or memo. But I knew that if I was to write a book for God, He would inspire me to do so. I agreed to write this book for Him.

During the next two years, God shared with me many different analogies and stories and gave me a new understanding of His Word. I wrote all of this down in a journal. Then Connie and I went through the Gospels, looking for everything that Jesus said about those who gain entrance to heaven. He had a lot to say on the subject. We found over fifty verses about this subject. Not one of them mentioned anything about saying a prayer to gain entrance to heaven.

I woke up one Saturday morning and greeted our Lord in prayer. He told me that today was the day I was going to write this book for Him. I said okay, sat at my computer, put my hands over the keyboard, and told God I was ready for Him to give me the words so I could type them up.

He said that He had already given me the words; he had been doing so over the previous two years. He said, "Look at that journal you've been writing." And I did. God showed me how to assemble what I had written in my journal into a book. At the end of that day, about 80 percent of this book was complete.

I believe God inspired me to write this book because He wanted us to understand that getting to heaven is not about our saying a prayer, or earning our salvation, or working our way there. It was about developing an intimate relationship with and having faith in Jesus Christ.

But before I start this book, I need to address two points. First, I'll be referring to the process of our repenting of our sins and receiving Jesus as our Lord and Savior as a "transaction." In doing so, it's not my intention to make fun or light of this very beautiful process; without our receiving the Holy Spirit through this process, nothing related to God's kingdom is possible. For the purposes of this book and the sake of discussion, though, I will call this a transaction.

Second, some of what I write in this book may seem very critical of the Christian church and its leaders. I can only imagine all the difficulties today's church leaders have to overcome to effectively manage and run their churches. Pastors, priests, and other leaders have so many roles to cover, such as counselor, administrator, husband, wife, mother, father, and friend. If what I say in this book is offensive to you as a church leader, I apologize, because that's not my intention. My intention is to bring to light something God has shown me; I believe what's being taught about salvation is not correct and is having a significant negative impact on the church.

What is being taught creates what I refer to as "casual Christians," those who walk with Jesus but casually. They look the same as all the other good, moral people in the world who are not Christians. I believe that Christians who diligently follow Jesus will look radically different from non-Christians. If we are following Him diligently, then the manifestation of the Holy Spirit through us will demonstrate things that those who aren't Christians cannot.

Thank you for taking the time to read this book. My prayers are that God will show Himself to you and that you will make your relationship with Jesus Christ your top priority.

I have provided a few review questions at the end of each chapter. These questions can be used in small group studies, Bible studies, or simply as questions you can explore with the Holy Spirit.

At the back of this book, I have also provided a short Bible study that goes over two chapters of the book of Matthew. I suggest that you study it before reading this book; it will help ground you in what Jesus said about your eternal life and give you some additional perspective.

CHAPTER 1

The Transaction

I remember the day as if it were yesterday.

About fifteen years ago, I was attending a Bible study group. The leader of the group regularly quoted part of Romans 8:13. He'd start the verse, "For if you live according to the sinful nature—" and everyone would join in and finish with "—you will die." It struck me as odd that believers would say that if we lived according to the sinful nature, we would die. I had always thought that if I believed in Jesus Christ and received Him as my Lord and Savior, I would live with Him in heaven for eternity. Why were they saying this? Sin led to death, they said.

After one meeting, I told the group leader I was confused about what he led the group to say. I told him I had been taught that if we believed in Jesus, said a prayer of repentance, and then acknowledged Him as our Lord and Savior, we would live in heaven for eternity with Him. The group leader told me that was correct. He thought about it for a moment and then said that he saw my point and he wouldn't be leading the group in saying that anymore.

To this day, his answer doesn't satisfy me. This was a seed of sorts that was planted in my heart. As it grew, it felt more and more uncomfortable. I knew God was stirring up my heart. I was curious and wanted to know what it took to have eternal life with God in heaven.

For much of my life, I had been taught that all I had to do was genuinely approach God and tell Him that I was a sinner who wanted to repent, turn from my sinful ways and live my life for Him. After that, I was to say a beautiful prayer about my belief in His Son, Jesus Christ, that He had been born of the Virgin Mary, and that He was crucified and died and, three days later, rose from the dead. At that moment, I'd receive God's gift of the Holy Spirit and would be born again, a new creation. After completing this process, I was in the Christian family; I would live with God, Jesus, and the Holy Spirit in heaven for eternity, along with everyone else who had done likewise. I had been taught nothing I could do would reverse this. "Once saved, always saved," they would say. Kind of like, "Do the transaction and you're in—once and done!"

I understand there are some Christian denominations that do not teach salvation through prayer. Instead, they might teach that salvation is sealed through some other one-time event, such as being baptized, accepting Jesus as your Lord and Savior, or something similar. They say, "Receive the Holy Spirit and you're part of the Christian family. You're in the Book of Life, and your eternal salvation is sealed."

I see this one-time-event concept of salvation being taught in our churches all the time, both directly and indirectly. For example, a church leader might invite those in attendance to say the sinner's prayer and to receive Jesus into their lives and hearts. Or a church leader will invite people to the altar and lead them in prayer or pray over them. After the event, the church leader will inform the people that they are new creations and have eternal life with Jesus. From that point on, they are encouraged to follow Jesus, but even if they don't follow Him diligently and do as He did, then from the standpoint of eternal life, that's okay because God is full of grace and mercy.

They say that salvation is a gift from God. It is because of God's grace, He chose to gift us with salvation and eternal life with Him in heaven. We don't deserve it, and there is nothing we can do to earn it.

I agree with all this, but I believe these words are taken out of context. Try looking at it this way: if our salvation is totally and completely due to what God does for us, we play no role in it and there is nothing we have to do to obtain it, then we must believe everyone is saved. But this conclusion is inconsistent with the Bible, which is clear on the point that some will enter heaven while others will spend eternity in hell.

So who goes to heaven and who goes to hell? Jesus will make this decision when He judges each of us. What will He base His decision on? Will it be on whether we experienced a one-time event, or something different?

I can't count how many people tell me things like, "I know I don't make my relationship with Jesus the priority that I should. But I'm busy, I have to work, my kids are involved in lots of activities, and I have things to do. I don't read the Bible (or don't read it as much as I should). I pray, but that's usually only before dinner." They say, "We live in a fallen world full of sin, and I'm a work in progress. I know God will forgive me because Jesus died for my sins."

These words feel to me like a cover-up for a lack of desire and effort. Just because God is full of grace and mercy doesn't excuse us from trying everything in our power to live according to the teachings of His Son.

When I listen closely and read between the lines of what's being taught at church, this is what I hear: After you complete the transaction, you don't have to make an effort to have a relationship with Jesus. You're going to heaven. You're encouraged to attend church, join a Bible study, serve others and give some money, but in terms of eternal life, it really doesn't matter; there's nothing at risk. God will forgive all your sins because of what Jesus did on the cross.

This concept of Christianity never rested well in my heart. I couldn't believe that this was how God had designed things. And yet our churches were teaching us that there's no risk in not diligently following Jesus after we've completed the transaction, so we can be casual in our pursuit of Him. We're going to heaven, so what does it matter if we don't make a strong effort?

Let me offer another perspective. At times, Jesus used a marriage analogy when describing His relationship with us. He referred to Himself as the Bridegroom, so we must be the bride. Do you wonder what kind of relationship Jesus might hope for between Himself and His bride?

Those who are married might better understand this. The wedding ceremony is a very special event, one that sets a covenant relationship in place. This is synonymous with doing the transaction or accepting Jesus as your Lord and Savior. But this is not the end of the relationship, nor even its peak; it's just the beginning. A close, personal, intimate relationship is supposed to be developed from that day on.

Time helps develop this relationship between a husband and wife, but for the most part, it develops through their decisions and deliberate actions to show love for one another. As they selflessly serve one another, work through tough day-to-day circumstances together, they will grow together, be bonded to one another, and walk together as one. As Paul put it, "The two shall become one."

So when Jesus comes back in all His glory and judges us to decide who goes to heaven and who goes to hell, what do you think He will base His judgment on? Will He ask only whether we got married to Him once upon a time? Or is it possible that He will judge us based on something else?

Is it possible He's looking for us to have a relationship with Him?

Review Questions

- What were you taught about salvation?
- Is Jesus your number one priority?
- If Jesus is not your number one priority, do you think it matters? If yes, then why do you think it matters?

CHAPTER 2

Walking the Plank

Today's view, "once saved, always saved," removes the risk of going to hell. A funny thing about risk is that we all behave differently when it is involved.

Think of it this way. What if someone told you that in order to get to heaven, you had to walk a mile on a plank only twenty-four inches wide? Let's say the plank was lying on the ground. Not too many would find this a challenge; the consequences of stepping off the plank would be minimal. If you messed up and stepped off of the plank, you could just step back on. It also wouldn't matter much if it was windy or if there were any other distractions. Nobody would be too concerned while walking the plank because there would be no risk involved; it's no big deal.

Let's change things. What if the plank were a thousand feet up in the air so that if you fell off, you'd die? I believe most people could still make this walk fairly easily; after all, it's still the same plank, twenty-four inches wide. But think about this walk: you wouldn't take it so casually. You'd pay attention to noises, lights, the wind, and any other distractions.

In this example, something's at risk, but not in the other. When there's risk, we pay more attention. Risk can change our behavior.

My wife Connie and I were riding our bikes one day. We live in Minnesota, and many of the bike trails are old, converted railroad beds. One particular section of the trail was elevated. It was probably twelve feet wide, but it was fifteen feet straight down on either side into all kinds of woods, thickets, and swamps. We started off in the afternoon. Keeping our bikes on the trail was no big deal; there was plenty of light, and we're good bike riders. Falling off the trail was not really a concern.

But soon, evening came, and with it, darkness. The small headlights on our bikes illuminated only the area directly in front of us, not the whole trail. I kept telling myself that this was the same trail we had ridden earlier, with no fear, but in the dark, things were different. We were anxious about falling off the side. Sometimes the trail turned, and we hoped to see the turns and not hit the swamp and ditch!

The difference between these two rides was the perceived risk and also our fear of falling into the thickets. Because we had some fear and perceived the risk to be higher, our attitude about the ride changed. We rode our bikes more slowly; we focused on the trail and paid closer attention to everything.

With this example in mind, think about your walk with Jesus today. Do you see it as a casual, risk-free walk?

Maybe it seems to have no risk because you believe what you were taught about salvation. Because you said a prayer and received the Holy Spirit of God, so you consider yourself saved and believe you will live eternally with Him in heaven. What is there to fear, and where is the risk in that? We've been taught that if we merely complete the transaction, what we do on earth after that moment has no impact on whether or not we get into heaven.

Some people will argue that this idea of the risk and fear of not going to heaven is only meant to scare them into having a relationship with God. I can understand that and I see why some people might believe this, but allow me to add some additional perspective. I don't see the problem with living with a healthy level of risk and fear. I can't count the number of times we are told in the Bible to fear God. Several hundred different verses speak about fearing God, fearing the Lord, or something very similar. Here are just a few:

> The fear of the Lord is the beginning of knowledge. (Proverbs 1:7)

> He said in a loud voice "Fear God" and give Him glory, because the hour of His judgment has come. (Revelation 14:7)

> And now Israel, what does the Lord your God ask of you but to fear the Lord your God, to walk in all His ways, to love Him, to serve the Lord your God with all your heart and with all your soul. (Deuteronomy 10:12)

But the eyes of the Lord are on those who fear him, on those whose hope is in His unfailing love to deliver them from death and keep them alive in famine. (Psalm 33:18)

Then the church throughout Judea, Galilee and Samaria enjoyed a time of peace. It was strengthened; and encouraged by the Holy Spirit, it grew in numbers, living in the fear of the Lord. (Acts 9:31)

Now all has been heard; here is the conclusion of the matter: Fear God and keep his commandments, for this is the whole duty of man. (Ecclesiastes 12:13)

Consider one of my favorite Bible heroes, Moses. He was a god-fearing man. Let's take a look at what he said to the Israelites after he came down from Mount Sinai with the Ten Commandments. First, though, let me first give you a little context. For a few months before Moses came down from Mount Sinai, the people had seen the presence of God covering the mountain with a dark cloud of smoke. They had seen thunder and lightning and heard the trumpets, and that frightened them. They kept a distance from the mountain and told Moses they didn't want to hear from God. They were afraid of Him and thought they might die.

That's when Moses told them, "God has come to test you, so that the fear of God will be with you to keep you from sinning" (Exodus 20:20). What do you think Moses meant when he said this? Do you think God wanted His people to be terrified of Him? I don't think so. God loves us and knows what's best for us. He knows how harmful sin is to us. God sets up boundaries of good behavior. He wants us to be fearful of the consequences of sin. He also wants us to have a certain level of fear, reverence, and respect for Him.

In Deuteronomy 5:29, God spoke to Moses about His hopes for His people as they prepared to travel to the Promised Land: "Oh, that their hearts would be inclined to fear me and keep all my commands always, so that it might go well with them and their children forever!" Listen to the heart of God. He wants to bless you and all His people. He loves us beyond comprehension and wants everyone to love Him back. He hopes our hearts will be inclined to fear Him and keep His commands.

But why would God say that He wants His people to fear Him? Fear is a word that has many uses and definitions. One definition of fear is awe, respect, and reverent obedience. I believe this is how the word *fear* is used in these verses. Maybe the following analogy will help. Think about a father and his children. The father creates rules and boundaries of behavior for his children. Some of them are intended to keep his children safe. For example, the father set a rule that his children must not play in the street. He does this because the children cannot and do not comprehend all the dangers of playing in the street. He also explains the consequences he will bring to bear if they are disobedient because he hopes this will prevent them from playing in the street and getting injured. Sometimes the fear of consequences keeps people from doing things they should not. In this example, do you think the father hopes his children are afraid of him because he told them he would punish them if they played in the street? I don't think so. But he probably hopes the children are fearful of the consequences and have some reverence and respect for him because they know he is fair and just and will carry out the consequences that he warned them about.

Isn't this what Moses was explaining in Exodus 20:20 and what God was saying in Deuteronomy 5:29? Aren't they really saying that having some fear of God and the consequences associated with sin might help keep us from sinning? The point is that a healthy level of fear might sometimes keep us from behaving inappropriately. If we believe that once saved, you're always saved, then there's no risk, no fear. From the standpoint of eternal life, if we believe this, then after doing the transaction, we're free to do whatever we want, without risk or fear of spending eternity in hell.

But what if they are wrong? What if our gaining entrance to heaven requires more than just saying a prayer and receiving Jesus? If that were true, wouldn't you want to know?

Review Questions

- What do you think it means to fear God?
- Why would God want us to fear Him?
- Do you believe God wants us to have a healthy level of fear of Him? Why or why not?

CHAPTER 3

Believe

Several years ago, Connie and I searched the Gospels for examples of Jesus talking about our entrance into heaven. We were amazed when we found over fifty of verses and parables that dealt with this topic. You know what? We didn't find a single verse that said anything like, "If you say a prayer or do a one-time event, you'll have eternal life." But we did find several verses that said those who believe in Jesus will have eternal life. I thought it would make sense to explore what the word *believe* means. Consider John 3:16, a well-known verse: "For God so loved the world that he gave his one and only Son, that whoever believes in him shall not perish but have eternal life."

I love this verse, and I'm grateful that it's so popular throughout the world today. But what does it really say about our entrance into heaven? It says that whoever believes in Him shall not perish, but have eternal life. Throughout the New Testament, we are urged to believe in Jesus, but what does believing in Christ really mean?

Many well-intentioned but mistaken Christians say that you believe if you think the stories in the Bible are true. Kind of like, "Believe the facts about Jesus, and you'll have eternal life." I disagree with this point of view. I think Jesus had something different in mind.

I have explored the word *believe* and found many definitions and uses. One definition is suppose, assume, or understand. For example, if someone tells you that he or she went to the shopping mall today, you might believe that; it's a casual acknowledgment. Other definitions go deeper than that. We have belief in things that determine who we are and what we do; we believe some matters so deeply that they drive our behavior. If you believe in the value of honesty, you'll be honest all the time, not just some of the time. Try thinking about it this way: If you say that you believe in something but your actions aren't consistent with that belief, people would challenge whether you really believe what you say you do. They'd think that you were not being honest with yourself, that you were trying to convince others you're someone you're not, or that you were in denial of who you really are and what you truly believe. If someone says they believe in Jesus Christ but they do not follow His teachings, then people may challenge whether that person really believes.

Visualize a rickety, old rope bridge that crosses a deep ravine. A fall from that height would mean certain death. You look at the bridge and wonder if it will support you. You see others crossing the bridge, so you believe it will hold you. But when you consider walking across it yourself, you recognize that something in your gut gives you caution. It's so easy to watch someone else walk across the bridge, but when it's your turn, you get weak knees and aren't so sure you trust it. Why is this? Would you say that you believe the bridge will support you because you saw others crossing? Maybe your belief is still in your head.

Let's go one step further. Now it's time for you to step onto the bridge and trust your life to its strength. This is the point where your belief goes from your head to your heart. Only when you walk across the bridge and completely trust and commit your life to it do you truly believe it will support you. With this example in mind, what do you think Jesus meant when in John 3:16 He talked about believing in Him and having eternal life? Was He referring to a belief we commit our lives to?

Sometimes when we believe in certain things, we develop new behaviors and abilities. For example, Jesus told us a few signs that will accompany those who believe in Mark 16:15–18.

> Go into all the world and preach the good news to all creation. Whoever believes and is baptized will be saved, but whoever does not believe will be condemned. And these signs will accompany those who believe: In my name they will drive out demons; they will speak in new tongues; they will pick up snakes with their hands; and when they drink deadly poison, it will not hurt them at all; they will place their hands on sick people, and they will get well.

There are a few things I want to touch on in this statement. First, Jesus said that to be saved, we need to believe and be baptized. I was baptized as an infant and as an adult, by complete immersion. Jesus was baptized, and God thought it was very good. I think it is important for Christians to be baptized. It's possible you are thinking that Jesus was referring to being baptized by receiving the Holy Spirit, and maybe He was. I don't have any more to say on this topic now, other than: if you haven't been baptized, you should strongly consider doing so.

Second, Jesus said that certain signs will accompany those who believe. They will do amazing things in His name, including driving out demons, speaking in new tongues, picking up snakes and drinking poison without being hurt, and placing their hands on sick people and healing them. I don't consider this an absolute or exhaustive list.

In this verse, Jesus was saying that if you believe in Him, you will do amazing things nonbelievers won't be able to. I think Jesus considered believers to be those who have not only completed the transaction and received the Holy Spirit but also allowed the Holy Spirit to manifest in their lives. Jesus was saying that if we believe, we will not look like everyone else. We who believe in Him will not blend in with non-Christians; we will look different and, with the power of the Holy Spirit, do things they cannot.

If you stood in a crowd of non-Christians who were good people living with high morals, would you stand out? You may say to yourself, yes, you would stand out because you attend church and they don't. This may be so, and it is different. But I'm asking whether the Holy Spirit is manifesting Himself in you. Are you doing miraculous things that non-Christians aren't doing? Using this as a possible guide to the meaning of believe, you might ask yourself: "Do I believe?"

Jesus is a teacher, the master, and we need to be students of the master. If we say we believe in Him, then it isn't sufficient to just have some knowledge and awareness of Him. As believers, we are to follow Him and put His teachings into action in our lives and develop a deep, personal, and intimate relationship with Him.

What do you think Jesus meant when He said those who believe in Him will have eternal life? Do you think He was talking about a casual belief, or something more? Let's take another look at the word *believe*. In Psalm 78, the psalmist wrote about the disbelief of the Israelites after God brought them out of Egypt. They had witnessed the plagues God placed on Pharaoh and all of Egypt. They witnessed the frightening night of the Passover, the parting of the Red Sea, water coming from rocks, manna from heaven, and pillars of smoke and fire to help guide them throughout the desert as they journeyed to the Promised Land.

These people had heard the voice of God. They asked Moses to speak with God because His voice frightened them, so I think it is safe to say that they believed God existed. They had witnessed His presence in numerous ways. But look at what was said about their belief, or lack thereof:

> In spite of all this, they kept on sinning; in
> spite of his wonders, they did not believe.
> So He ended their days in futility and their
> years in terror. Whenever God slew them,
> they would seek Him; they eagerly turned

to Him again. They remembered that God was their Rock, that God Most High was their Redeemer. But then they would flatter Him with their mouths, lying to Him with their tongues; their hearts were not loyal to Him, they were not faithful to His covenant. (Psalm 78:32–37)

Look at how the psalmist used the word *believe*. Do you think the Israelites didn't believe in God? Remember all the wonders they had witnessed. And yet they turned from Him and worshipped other things, other gods. They disobeyed God; they didn't follow Him. The psalmist called this unbelief.

Let's take a look at another verse from the Old Testament, but first let me give you a little context. God asked Moses to have each of the twelve Israelite tribes supply a leader to explore part of the Promised Land. The twelve went exploring as requested. They found that the land was lush and flowing with milk and honey, just as God had promised. But when they returned to give their report, ten of the twelve on the journey started to exaggerate about the people who lived in the land. They said the people were powerful and their cities were fortified.

The other two, Caleb and Joshua, tried to tell the Israelites that through God's strength, they could conquer these people, but the ten continued with their exaggerations. They said the inhabitants were strong and so huge that they made the explorers look like grasshoppers in comparison.

Caleb and Joshua knew that the people who inhabited the land were a force to be reckoned with, but their faith in God was stronger. They knew these people were nothing compared to their God. They knew God could and would deliver them if they attacked. But those who assembled to hear this report didn't listen to Caleb and Joshua; they believed the other ten. Because of those exaggerated stories, the whole Israelite community lost their faith in God and no longer believed that He could and would deliver them to the Promised Land. They regretted leaving Egypt in the first place. They wanted to choose a new leader and return to Egypt. They also wanted to stone Moses, Joshua, and Caleb. The situation infuriated God. Let's see what He thought about the Israelites' belief in Him.

> But the whole assembly talked about stoning them. Then the glory of the Lord appeared at the tent of meeting to all the Israelites. The Lord said to Moses, "How long will these people treat me with contempt? How long will they refuse to believe in me, in spite of all the signs I have performed among them? I will strike them down with a plague and destroy them, but I will make you into a nation greater and stronger than they." (Numbers 14:11–12)

Look at how God used the word *believe*. He was tired of their contempt. They had said they would follow God, but they didn't. When life got hard and they feared for their lives, they turned to God, but when their calamities were lifted, they turned from Him. God knew the Israelites didn't believe in Him or that He could and would do what He had promised. This was not about an awareness of God or a casual acknowledgement of Him; it was about the status of their trust and faith in and relationship with God.

My hope is that you are expanding your view of the word *believe*, especially in terms of how Jesus used it in John 3:16 and many other places in the Bible. What if Jesus was saying that believing in Him meant you

- allowed the Holy Spirit to manifest Himself in you;
- could do things non-Christians couldn't do;
- strived to live the way Jesus taught us to live; and
- followed Him with all your heart, mind, body, and soul?

Review Questions

- What do you think it means to *believe* in Jesus Christ?
- In Numbers 14:11, The Lord said, "How long will they refuse to believe in me, in spite of all the miraculous signs I have performed among them." What do you think God meant when He used the word *believe* in this verse? Is this the same definition that Jesus used in John 3:16?

CHAPTER 4

Grace and Works

Christians have wrestled for many years about the relationship between their works, God's grace, and how it all relates to their eternal life. Many people say that if your equation for eternal salvation involves anything besides Jesus, you're suggesting that Christians earn their way to heaven. They say this because they believe God has already done everything to save you. Once you complete the transaction, your eternal life in heaven is sealed up, your name is in the Book of Life, and nothing you can do will reverse this. They say the one and only reason we are saved is because God is good and full of grace and mercy. God did it all; we have nothing to do and no role to play in it. However, I disagree with that view. I believe we do play some type of a role. Please allow me to explain why.

In regards to eternal salvation, God made two covenants with us. The first (the old covenant) involved obedience to the law. The second (the new covenant) is having faith in Jesus Christ.

In the old covenant with God, no one could remain in a right-standing relationship with Him. The Israelites would sin and then have to sacrifice something to get back into a right-standing relationship with God. Then they would sin again and have to sacrifice again. If you've spent much time studying the Old Testament, you know what I mean. God told them they had to sacrifice various animals, including sheep, goats, oxen, and birds, to atone for their sins and pay the penalty for them. God knew that they couldn't attain perfect adherence to His law; everyone fell short. He knew their sacrifices were not perfect, so they had to be repeated.

During this time, God's people continued to sin and to fail to adhere to His law. Some of them worshiped other gods and, at times, did many things that were detestable in His eyes. In spite of all that, while they were still steeped in sin, God gave an amazing display of His love by sending His Son to earth to be with us and die a gruesome death on the cross to atone for our sins. Jesus was the perfect, final sacrifice that had to be made for humanity's sins.

After God raised Jesus from the depths of hell to ascend to heaven, He left us the Holy Spirit and made a brand-new covenant with us. God's unfathomable sacrifice created a new path to Him and made a way for us to get into a right-standing relationship with Him. God did all the work creating this new way. We didn't deserve this new path, and we did nothing to earn it. We had nothing to do with it and played no role in developing it. Because of God's grace, mercy, and absolute, crazy love for us, He created this new path for us. Because of what He did, we can now believe in Jesus, have faith in Him, and be in a right-standing relationship with God. But remember this very important point: It's not just about coming to the path. We must walk it. The walking part is how we live here and now. Maybe the following illustration will help.

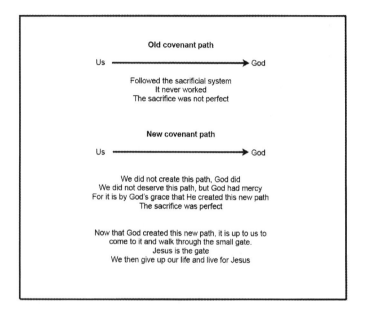

Try to put yourself in the place of the Jews in Jesus's time. They had been following God's laws for several thousand years before Jesus was born. Because of the old covenant with God, they believed that by following (or obeying) the law, they would be in a right-standing relationship with Him. This belief was ingrained in their hearts and minds as it was passed on from generation to generation. For thousands of years, this was how it was; there was no other way. Their salvation was dependent on their works of following God's law.

But while all this was going on, Jesus came along and changed everything. A belief in Jesus replaced following the law. The Israelites had to let go of their deeply entrenched belief that their works based approach of following the law would save them. In its place, they were to accept that their eternal salvation would come from having faith in Jesus. This was a hard concept for the Jews of that time to accept. Even though new believers in Christ were freed from their works based salvation, their old nature and their old habit of doing works did not easily die in their hearts. Those who professed a faith in Jesus still had to be repeatedly taught that their salvation was no longer based on performing God's laws.

God created the new path (the new covenant) out of His grace, mercy, and love for us. Our salvation is no longer dependent on our working to be obedient to the law of the old covenant; instead, we need to follow the path of God's grace. Following this new path of grace requires a belief in and personal relationship with Jesus Christ. Remember this important fact. God created this new path, but now it is up to us to walk it.

Now that you have this background about the old and new covenants, let's take a look at a very popular verse, Ephesians 2:8–9: "For it is by grace you have been saved, through faith—and this not from yourselves, it is the gift of god—not by works, so that no one can boast." Many Christian leaders misinterpret and misuse this verse to support their view that God has done everything and we have nothing to contribute to our spending eternity in heaven. They say that our salvation is the gift of God, not the result of works. They believe this statement supports their argument that it is all God and we play no role in it. They say that if we do play any sort of role in our own salvation, then we are advocating a works-based salvation. I disagree with their interpretation of this verse. Let me explain why.

When you read the entire letter Paul wrote to the Ephesians, you can see that he is reminding the churches of Ephesus that their focus should be on the new covenant, not the old covenant. When Paul says, "for it is by grace you have been saved, through faith," he is reminding them that God created the new covenant because of His grace and their salvation now comes from the new covenant. Paul then continues by saying "not by works, so that no one can boast", which means that the old works based approach of salvation is no longer the focus. Back in the days of the Old Testament, the Pharisees and other religious leaders of the time would brag about their success in following all the laws. That is why Paul said, "so that no one can boast".

When Paul wrote this letter, he was addressing a group of believers. He was reminding them that God created the new covenant because of His grace, not because we were good or that we deserved it and that their eternal salvation in heaven would not come from following the works based approach of the old covenant, but from the new covenant. Their eternal salvation can only come from having faith in Jesus Christ.

Let's switch topics a little and now roll forward two thousand years and talk about current times. In America today, we have different struggles than those in Ephesus did. I believe one problem is how we put ourselves first. Sometimes, our attitude is, "I don't need a God to guide me and tell me how to run my life, just one to give me eternal life and make my life easy and prosperous." We tend to figure out life on our own terms, following our own determined ways rather than following Jesus. We tend to do whatever seems right to us and make God a part-time activity. We get busy and justify all the distractions we've let into our lives. We struggle to fit God into our busy schedules. We set our agendas and ask God to bless them. This is not how it was meant to be. Jesus must be the focus and center of our lives. All we do should flow from our relationship with Him. We are to live lives that are completely dependent on Him in all we do.

Let's look at a statement from Oswald Chambers' daily devotion, *My Utmost for His Highest* (October 19).

> The great enemy of the Lord Jesus Christ today is the idea of practical work that has no basis in the New Testament but comes from the systems of the world. This work insists upon endless energy and activities, but no private life with God. The emphasis is put on the wrong thing ... An active Christian worker too often lives to be seen by others, while it is the innermost, personal area that reveals the power of a person's life.
>
> We must get rid of the plague of the spirit of this religious age in which we live. In our Lord's life was none of the pressure and the rushing of tremendous activity that we regard so highly today, and a disciple is to be like His Master. The central

point of the kingdom of Jesus Christ is a
personal relationship with Him, not public
usefulness to others.

Think about this. So many material and worldly things
distract us from Jesus. Today, we seem to rely on our own
strength to get through the day as opposed to the power and
strength of the Holy Spirit. Jesus is to be our main focus all
day long, every day. He expects total commitment. Jesus
expects us to live servants' lives, lives that are dependent on
Him for everything.

Being completely honest, would you say that you are
trying to live a life completely dependent on Jesus? Do you
allow Jesus to reign in your heart? Doing this requires you
to make a decision based on the question, "Will I die to
myself and allow Jesus to live in me?" Jesus lets us make this
decision. The choice is ours.

When you think about your decision to follow Jesus
and consider God's grace, remember that it was by God's
grace that He created a new way to get into a right-standing
relationship with Him. We did nothing to create this new
way; God did it all. We didn't deserve to have Him do this;
we were all sinners. But now that God has done His part, we
have to do ours by receiving Jesus in our hearts, following
Him, and developing a relationship with Him.

Developing a relationship with Jesus and following
Him will require work, effort, commitment, intention,
and desire. But in doing this work, we aren't "working"
our way to heaven; rather, we're putting in the effort to
develop a relationship with Jesus. Let's not kid ourselves,
developing a relationship with Jesus will be difficult and will

also probably cause many hardships in our lives. Jesus said it would cost us everything.

Remember it this way: Because of God's amazing grace, He created a new path for us to get into a right-standing relationship with Him (the new covenant.) That new path is to believe in His Son. Now it is up to us to walk it. And yes, walking this new path does require work.

May God strengthen you and bless you as you walk with Him on this new path!

Review Questions

- Try to put yourself back in time, when the Jews learned about the end of the old covenant and the beginning of the new covenant. What do you think it was like for them to hear this and change their beliefs?
- What do you think it means to walk the path of the new covenant?

CHAPTER 5

The Cost of Following

One day, I was reading the book of John and I ran across this statement made by Jesus: "If anyone does not remain in me, he is like a branch that is thrown away and withers; such branches are picked up, thrown into the fire and burned" (John 15:6). This verse stirred up something in me. I wondered what Jesus meant when He said, "does not remain in me…thrown into the fire and burned." This seemed to go against the idea that once we say the prayer, we are in. When Jesus said, "remain in me" is it possible that He was describing a one-time event or is it more likely that He was describing how we live our lives?

Then I read Paul's letter to the Galatians (5:19–20).

> The acts of the sinful nature are obvious: sexual immorality, impurity and debauchery; idolatry and witchcraft; hatred, discord, jealousy, fits of rage, selfish

> ambition, dissensions, factions and envy;
> drunkenness, orgies, and the like. I warn
> you, as I did before, that those who live like
> this will not inherit the kingdom of God.

This Scripture clearly states that if I choose to live a sinful life, I will not inherit the kingdom of God. At first, I wondered if Paul had been writing to non-Christians, trying to let them know that if they didn't repent of their sins and accept Jesus as their Lord and Savior, they would live in hell for eternity. I read the passage again, but this time, I started reading earlier in Galatians and noticed the words, "to the churches in Galatia" (Galatians 1:2). This puzzled me because if the Galatians had already said the prayer, why would they have to worry about sinning and spending eternity in hell? Was it possible that what I had been taught all my life about the road to salvation was not right? Was there more to gaining entrance into heaven than just doing the transaction? I went back to John and read more of what Jesus said.

> For the Father loves the Son and shows him
> all he does. Yes, to your amazement he will
> show him even greater things than these.
> For just as the Father raises the dead and
> gives them life, even so the Son gives life to
> whom he is pleased to give it.

> Moreover, the Father judges no one, but has
> entrusted all judgment to the Son, that all
> may honor the Son just as they honor the

Father. He who does not honor the Son
does not honor the Father, who sent him.

I tell you the truth, whoever hears my word
and believes him who sent me has eternal life
and will not be condemned; he has crossed
over from death to life. (John 5:20–24)

This Scripture tells us that God gave Jesus the responsibility
and authority to judge us. I thought, *Okay, this is good. Jesus
will be the judge.* I also understood that if I heard the words
Jesus said and believed He was sent to earth by God, then
I would cross over from death to life. I assumed that this
meant I would live in heaven with God for eternity. This
made me feel better; it sounded more like what was taught in
church. But it still didn't resolve things for me. I had many
more questions. I kept reading.

For as the Father has life in himself, so he
has granted the Son to have life in himself.
And he has given him authority to judge
because he is the Son of Man.

Do not be amazed at this, for a time is
coming when all who are in their graves
will hear his voice and come out—those
who have done good will rise to live, and
those who have done evil will rise to be
condemned. (John 5:26–29)

God has life and granted Jesus the same life; Jesus has
the authority to judge because God gave Him that authority.

Jesus said those who have done good will rise to live and those who have done evil will rise to be condemned.

What's interesting is what Jesus didn't say. He didn't say that those who have said a prayer will rise to live and those who haven't will be condemned; no, He said those who have done good or evil will rise to either live or be condemned. I wondered if Jesus was telling us the kinds of things He will judge when He decides who goes to heaven and who goes to hell. Do you think He will determine who does good versus evil?

This raised even more questions for me, so I brought them to God and prayed about them. I just love God's response to me. He said, "Good question. Keep reading my Word, and you'll find your answer. Seek these questions with all your heart."

That's what I did. I went to Matthew 19:16–30 to read about the rich young man.

> Now a man came up to Jesus and asked, "Teacher, what good thing must I do to get eternal life?" "Why do you ask me about what is good?" Jesus replied. "There is only One who is good. If you want to enter life, obey the commandments."

> "Which ones?" the man inquired. Jesus replied, "'Do not murder, do not commit adultery, do not steal, do not give false testimony, honor your father and mother,' and 'love your neighbor as yourself.'"

"All these I have kept," the young man said. "What do I still lack?" Jesus answered, "If you want to be perfect, go, sell your possessions and give to the poor, and you will have treasure in heaven. Then come, follow me." When the young man heard this, he went away sad, because he had great wealth.

Then Jesus said to his disciples, "I tell you the truth, it is hard for a rich man to enter the kingdom of heaven. Again I tell you, it is easier for a camel to go through the eye of a needle than for a rich man to enter the kingdom of God."

When the disciples heard this, they were greatly astonished and asked, "Who then can be saved?" Jesus looked at them and said, "With man this is impossible, but with God all things are possible."

Peter answered him, "We have left everything to follow you! What then will there be for us?" Jesus said to them, "I tell you the truth, at the renewal of all things, when the Son of Man sits on his glorious throne, you who have followed me will also sit on twelve thrones, judging the twelve tribes of Israel.

And everyone who has left houses or brothers or sisters or father or mother or children or fields for my sake will receive a hundred times as much and will inherit eternal life. But many who are first will be last, and many who are last will be first."

This is a great story about someone who thought he could get to heaven by following the rules, or as some would say, by working his way to heaven. He was totally focused on the old covenant, which was to follow the law to get into a right-standing relationship with God. Jesus was very clear with this young man. He saw that his great wealth had separated him from Jesus, so He told the rich man to sell everything, give to the poor, and follow Him. But the rich young man chose not to do what Jesus said, and he walked away sad. I hope you notice that Jesus didn't chase after him and try to convince him that he was making the wrong decision and that his life on earth was nothing compared to eternal life with Jesus. The rich young man had made his decision. Jesus just let him go.

Think about this for a minute. If gaining entrance to heaven really is as simple as doing the transaction, then why didn't Jesus just say so? The man was obviously rich and could have been a great advocate for Jesus. Why didn't Jesus tell him to do the transaction?

If one believes that salvation comes from doing the transaction, he or she will find the next part of this story even more puzzling. When the young man left, Jesus told His disciples that it is difficult for a rich man to enter the kingdom of heaven. In fact, He said that it is easier for a camel to go through the eye of a needle than for a rich man to enter the kingdom of God. Why is it so hard? Couldn't a rich man also say the prayer of salvation to enter heaven? I mean, how hard is it to say the prayer?

If going to heaven is as simple as accepting Jesus as Lord and Savior, saying a prayer, and accepting the gift of the Holy Spirit, then why did Jesus say it was so hard? Could there be more to having eternal life with God than just accepting Jesus and saying the prayer?

What if Jesus expects us to live our lives completely dependent on Him, not upon our material possessions, in order to gain entrance to heaven? If so, Jesus's comment about the difficulty of entering the kingdom of God makes more sense. On the other hand, if all we have to do is say the prayer, then what Jesus said seems to make no sense.

I first said the prayer when I was ten, and I've said it many times since then. Therefore, I'm saved and will live with God in heaven for eternity—right? If this is true, then it shouldn't be hard for me to enter the kingdom of God. Aren't we taught in church that God does all the work and all we have to do is say the prayer and accept Jesus? Then what's so difficult?

Remember: Jesus didn't just say that entering heaven is difficult; He compared it to how hard it would be for a camel to go through the eye of a needle. At this point in my reading, I started to have serious doubts about what I had been taught about salvation. None of it lined up with what I was reading in the Bible. I wondered if there was more to know about gaining everlasting life.

In Matthew 19:29, Jesus said that everyone who has left houses or brothers or sisters or father or mother or children or fields for His sake will receive a hundred times as much and inherit eternal life. Notice what He asked us to do: leave everything and follow Him. He didn't say that following Him would be a casual event; rather, He set a very high standard for following Him.

In Luke 9:57–62, Jesus said it would cost us something to follow Him.

> As they were walking along the road, a man said to him, "I will follow you wherever you go." Jesus replied, "Foxes have holes and birds of the air have nests, but the Son of Man has no place to lay his head." He said to another man, "Follow me." But the man replied, "Lord, first let me go and bury my father."
>
> Jesus said to him, "Let the dead bury their own dead, but you go and proclaim the kingdom of God." Still another said, "I will follow you, Lord; but first let me go back and say good-by to my family." Jesus replied, "No one who puts his hand to the plow and looks back is fit for service in the kingdom of God."

When I first read this, I wondered why Jesus had been so rude. He was obviously not doing a very good job of marketing Himself. Who would want to follow Him? But think about this passage for a minute. Jesus was being very real here. He was telling us that following Him would not be easy. He knew many would choose not to follow Him.

And those who did could expect to have trouble of all kinds as they walked in His teachings. It would cost people something very significant to follow Him. Look at Jesus's response to the man who asked to follow Him: "The Son of Man has no place to rest His head." I think Jesus was saying that following Him would require much work and probably a lot of discomfort.

Some people said they were willing to follow Him, but had a few things to take care of first. Jesus responded by saying that the dead should bury their own dead. Jesus had very high expectations for those who considered themselves followers. He did not say, "Okay, no problem. Come follow me after you get all your other things done." He told them to drop everything and follow Him. Jesus wants to be our first priority.

Look at how Jesus closed this verse: "No one who puts his hand to the plow and looks back is fit for service in the kingdom of God." With these words, Jesus was not saying, "Just complete that transaction and you're in." I am hearing something very different: Jesus wants a commitment.

Let's take a look at Matthew 4, when Jesus calls His first disciples. Jesus first saw Peter and his brother Andrew. They were busy fishing, casting their nets into the water. Jesus told them, "Come follow me." At once, they left their nets and followed him. Then Jesus saw James and his brother John. They were in a boat with their father, preparing their fishing nets. Jesus called them; they immediately left the boat and their father and followed Him.

As you think about Jesus calling these four disciples, please consider this: Peter, Andrew, James, and John were all fishermen. Back in those days, it was traditional that the profession of the father would be taken over by his children. Imagine for a moment what was going through the minds of these four young men when Jesus called them. They are out fishing, making a living, learning a trade from their fathers, and all of a sudden, here comes Jesus. He says, "Follow me," and they immediately give up everything and follow Him!

What do you think it was like for them to make this decision? Think about what they gave up. What do you think their fathers thought about their decision? Who would take over the family business? What do you think their friends and families thought about their decision? Is this the kind of sacrifice and commitment Jesus may expect from us?

Last, let's consider Jesus's words about strict discipline.

> If your right eye causes you to sin, gouge it out and throw it away. It is better for you to lose one part of your body than for your whole body to be thrown into hell.

> And if your right hand causes you to sin, cut it off and throw it away. It is better for you to lose one part of your body than for your whole body to go into hell. (Matthew 5:29–30)

Jesus wasn't literally saying that you have to gouge out your eye or cut off your hand; He knew how important our hands and eyes were to us. He was making the point that we are better off getting rid of whatever it is that causes us to sin, even if it's a hand or an eye. Jesus set very high standards for those who believe and claim to be His followers. Do you think that when Jesus judges whether we lived like we believed, his standards will be this high? What if they are?

Review Questions

- Jesus said it was hard for a rich man to enter the kingdom of God. What do you think He meant?
- In Luke 9:62, Jesus said, "No one who puts his hand to the plow and looks back is fit for service in the kingdom of God." What do you think He meant by this?
- What has following Jesus cost you?

CHAPTER 6

Entrance into Heaven

I have collected many statements from Jesus and a few parables from the Gospels that speak of gaining entrance to heaven. None of them says anything about reciting a prayer or performing a single, one-time action to get into heaven.

Let's start with Matthew 5:20: "For I tell you that unless your righteousness surpasses that of the Pharisees and the teachers of the law, you will certainly not enter the kingdom of heaven." In Jesus's day, the Pharisees were the authority on God; they studied His Word and helped His people understand and interpret what He wanted of them. But by the time Jesus came, God was not pleased with the Pharisees. They had manipulated His intentions so that they would benefit and be glorified. Jesus said they were clean and pretty on the outside, but rotten inside. So, to gain entrance to heaven, our righteousness has to surpass that of the Pharisees.

In Matthew 5:22, Jesus spoke about keeping resentments and being angry with others. He said, "But I tell you that anyone who is angry with a brother or sister will be subject to judgment. Again, anyone who says to a brother or sister, 'Raca,' is answerable to the court. And anyone who says, 'You fool!' will be in danger of the fire of hell." Why would just calling someone a fool put us in danger of the fire of hell? Once saved, aren't we always saved?

Jesus loves us all very much, even the little children. Look at what He says about them in Matthew 18:3–5.

> And he said: "I tell you the truth, unless you change and become like little children, you will never enter the kingdom of heaven. Therefore, whoever humbles himself like this child is the greatest in the kingdom of heaven. And whoever welcomes a little child like this in my name welcomes me."

Why must we be like little children to enter the kingdom of heaven? Maybe Jesus meant that our trust in Him must be similar to the trust little ones have in those who care for them. Maybe our faith in Jesus must be similar to the faith children have in their parents. So, to enter heaven, we need to have faith like a child's. Would you characterize your faith in Jesus as similar to a three-year-old's trust and faith in their parents?

I found another statement from Jesus about little children that is similar to what He said in Matthew. This one comes from Mark 10:14–15.

> When Jesus saw this, he was indignant. He said to them, "Let the little children come to me, and do not hinder them, for the kingdom of God belongs to such as these. Truly I tell you, anyone who will not receive the kingdom of God like a little child will never enter it."

Will we receive the kingdom of God like a little child? And does it matter if we don't?

In this next verse, Jesus said that He expected us to keep watching for His return and to be ready because He will come at a time when we are not expecting Him.

> The Lord answered, "Who then is the faithful and wise manager, whom the master puts in charge of his servants to give them their food allowance at the proper time? It will be good for that servant whom the master finds doing so when he returns. I tell you the truth, he will put him in charge of all his possessions.
>
> But suppose the servant says to himself, 'My master is taking a long time in coming,' and he then begins to beat the menservants and maidservants and to eat and drink and get drunk. The master of that servant will come on a day when he does not expect him and at an hour he is not aware of. He will cut him to pieces and assign him a place with the unbelievers." (Luke 12:42–46)

I wonder why Jesus said this. From the standpoint of eternal life, does it matter whether we are doing what He asked us when He returns? What if it does matter? If we don't live our lives in expectation of His return, always being on the watch, will it impact our entrance to heaven? What does Jesus say will happen to the faithful and wise manager if he stops doing what he was supposed to do? He will cut him to pieces and place him with the unbelievers.

Jesus seemed to be confirming His prior usage of the word *believe*. If we believe in Jesus, we should be living as though we believe in him. If we don't live this way, then we probably don't really believe. It is not a casual belief that He calls us to.

This next statement of Jesus's is interesting. In Mark 13:12–13, Jesus told His disciples what it would be like at the end of the age: "Brother will betray brother to death, and a father his child. Children will rebel against their parents and have them put to death. All men will hate you because of me, but he who stands firm to the end will be saved" (Mark 13:12–13).

From an earthly standpoint, Jesus didn't describe a pretty scene; the end of the age feels and sounds like a rather tough time. I believe Jesus was saying that if we truly live our lives for Him, we will be persecuted for it. This persecution can come from some of the people whom we thought loved us. Last, I hope you've noticed what Jesus said about those who stand firm to the end: He said they would be saved. Was Jesus saying that, if we choose to turn away from our faith in Him because of the trials we encounter, we will not be saved? I believe that is exactly what he is saying.

Let's look at Luke 14:25–35, in which Jesus said that following Him would not be an easy journey; we will have troubles.

Large crowds were traveling with Jesus, and turning to them he said: "If anyone comes to me and does not hate his father and mother, his wife and children, his brothers and sisters—yes, even his own life—he cannot be my disciple. And anyone who does not carry his cross and follow me cannot be my disciple.

Suppose one of you wants to build a tower. Will he not first sit down and estimate the cost to see if he has enough money to complete it? For if he lays the foundation and is not able to finish it, everyone who sees it will ridicule him, saying, 'This fellow began to build and was not able to finish.'

Or suppose a king is about to go to war against another king. Will he not first sit down and consider whether he is able with ten thousand men to oppose the one coming against him with twenty thousand? If he is not able, he will send a delegation while the other is still a long way off and will ask for terms of peace.

In the same way, any of you who does not give up everything he has cannot be my disciple. Salt is good, but if it loses its saltiness, how can it be made salty again? It is fit neither for the soil nor for the manure

pile; it is thrown out. He who has ears to
hear, let him hear."

It seems that Jesus was taking things to a new level. Have
you ever wondered why Jesus would tell you to hate your
mother and father? I don't think He meant this literally. He
was trying to delineate the large gap between the quality and
intimacy of our relationship with Him versus our relationships
with anyone else, including our mother and father. He not
only wanted to be first, He wanted to be first by a long way.
Our relationship with Him needs to be our top priority.

If Jesus is our number one relationship, we will think
of Him and consider His ways in all we do—more than we
will of our work, spouse, children, or friends. If you were
to honestly evaluate your own life, your desires, and your
priorities, would you conclude that Jesus was your number
one relationship? Do you really give Jesus your everything?

Jesus told us it would cost us everything (from an earthly
standpoint) to have this relationship with Him. Have you
considered this? What do you suppose Jesus meant when
told us to give up everything? Did He mean that we are to
sell everything and give to the poor? Maybe, maybe not. It
is more likely that He was calling us to give up our lives as
we know them and let Him determine what we do in life.

Are you willing to do this? What would your life be like
if you truly followed Jesus? Would you have the same job?
Would you live in the same house, or even the same state?
Would your activities, such as sports, capture as much of
your attention and time as they do now?

In John 3:3, Jesus makes a great statement about being
born again: "Jesus replied, 'Very truly I tell you, no one can

see the kingdom of God unless he is born again.'" Jesus said we must be born again to see the kingdom of God. What does it mean to be born again? Aren't we born again after we do the transaction and receive Jesus into our hearts? Jesus said this was a requirement for seeing the kingdom of heaven. But we have been reading more of what Jesus said, so surely we can see that this is not the only requirement. Maybe it's just the beginning.

Jesus had much to say about who gains entrance into heaven. He expects us to turn from our life of sin (repent) and turn over our will and life to His care. When we do this, we receive the gift of the Holy Spirit. But that is not the end; it's just the beginning. Now that we have the Holy Spirit, Jesus expects us to use the gifts of the Holy Spirit to beat down the gates of hell. He expects us to follow Him, love others, serve others, teach others about Him, and love God with all our heart, mind, body, and soul.

What did Jesus say about our gaining entrance to heaven if we don't live this way? How will He judge us if He returns to find we are not living to the standard He set for us? Think about this for a minute: What if it takes more than just doing the transaction to get into heaven? What if this is one of the greatest deceptions Satan has pulled off? Perhaps the Devil has convinced our church leaders and many other Christians that all we have to do is say the sinner's prayer (i.e., complete the transaction) to gain entrance into heaven. So, what if they're wrong?

What if we stand before Jesus and He says, "It's a shame you listened to what they said. You should have been listening to me and following the Holy Spirit. You should have paid more attention to what was written in your Bible.

You should have known that the hearts of men are sinful in nature."

I'm not accusing anyone of intentionally leading us astray, just that they may be mistaken. And if they are wrong, wouldn't you want to know? Remember: you are the one who will have to stand before Jesus and answer to Him. You will not be able to direct the blame onto someone else. You will be responsible for your own answers.

If you could hit the reset button and have a do-over, would you want one? When you come before Jesus and hear His judgment, it will then be too late. The time to change is now.

Think about this: What is Jesus going to ask you and how are you going to respond?

Review Questions

- In Matthew 18:3, Jesus said, "unless you change and become like little children, you will never enter the kingdom of heaven." What do you think Jesus meant?
- In Luke 14:33, Jesus said that, to be His disciple, we have to give up everything we have. What do you think Jesus meant by this?
- Does Jesus promise those who follow Him to be provided food, water, and comfort? Why or why not?

CHAPTER 7

Our Close Relationship

I want to summarize what's been discussed so far. The question I've been trying to answer relates to spending eternity in heaven. Jesus will one day judge us worthy of heaven or condemn us to hell. What will be the basis of His decision? What will Jesus look at in our lives when He makes His decision? Will He look back to determine whether we made a decision one day to accept Him as our Lord and Savior, to repent of our sins, to say a prayer acknowledging Him as the Son of God and Lord of our lives, to receive Him into our hearts and receive the gift of the Holy Spirit? Will He judge us based on whether we did this transaction once upon a time? Or, will He judge the quality of the relationship He has with us, how we lived, and how we worked our faith into our lives? Will Jesus look not only at whether we did the transaction but also at what we did with our lives afterward? Will he base His judgment on more than just whether we received Him into our hearts one day? Is it really true that, once saved, you're always saved?

It seems to me that Jesus will judge whether we lived our lives as His followers, whether we lived faith-filled lives according to the Holy Spirit and brought His power to bear in our circumstances. He will determine whether we lived our lives as He instructed.

When Jesus returns, will He say that He has a close, personal, and intimate relationship with you? What does it mean to have such a relationship with Jesus? Here's something to think about when considering your answer.

Let's say you were interested in someone who is very popular and you have followed his life. Let's also say that there is much information available about him. Maybe this person is a great leader, like the president of a great nation. Because you want to know him, you have read everything written about him and watched every video and movie about him. You believe you know everything there is to know about this person. But would you now conclude that you have a relationship with him? If you walked up to that person on the street and shook his hand, would he know you? Could you really consider yourself to have any kind of relationship with him?

We can all agree that knowing everything about someone is different from having a relationship with him. So if you read the Bible, attend church, participate in a Bible study, behave with the highest of moral standards, and serve the poor, does that mean you have a relationship with Jesus? Maybe—but then again, maybe not.

I guess the real question is whether you do these activities *with* Jesus. When you do these things, do you at the same time consider Him, follow the promptings of the Holy Spirit, and enjoy being in His presence? Do you listen to Him and for Him as you do these activities? If you do, it's starting to sound more like having a relationship with Him, rather than just having knowledge of Him. If, during all your activities, you are not doing them with Jesus, then you may be doing a whole lot of good things, but you aren't developing a relationship with Jesus.

Let's say you decide to spend a week with your best friend from out of town. You spend the entire week with him (physically in his presence), but never talk to him, interact with him, or introduce him to anyone. You know your friend exists and that he's with you, but if you're not interacting with him, you're certainly not developing a relationship with him. This would be weird behavior, indeed.

But in fact, is this how you sometimes treat Jesus? You know Jesus said He would always be with you, but are you failing to pay attention to Him, interact with Him, and introduce Him to anyone? I have days like that, and I hate it. I don't like admitting this, but it's true. And yes, it scares me. It makes me want to run back to Jesus and ask for His forgiveness and repent of my evil ways.

Maybe you're thinking, *I go to church and am in a Bible study, so that's good enough.* It's not a question of good enough, however, but of whether the Holy Spirit is alive in you and working in your heart, and whether the things you do are manifestations of God's love in you. You may be doing good, but if you're doing so with your own strength instead of the outpouring of your heart, it's possible you're just doing good but not developing a relationship with Jesus.

I believe Jesus is calling us to a deep, close, and personal relationship with Him, in which He doesn't play second fiddle to anyone. He expects us to keep our relationship with Him number one. I think most Christians understand this, but we're taught, "once saved, always saved," which suggests there's no risk or consequence to intentionally ignoring Jesus and the promptings of the Holy Spirit. But what if Jesus said that the consequences of not developing a personal relationship with Him are that you cannot go to heaven? Would you then change your walk with Him? Would you live your life differently?

Let's look at some more of what Jesus said in Matthew 7:21–23.

> Not everyone who says to me, "Lord, Lord," will enter the kingdom of heaven, but only he who does the will of my Father who is in heaven. Many will say to me on that day, "Lord, Lord, did we not prophesy in your name, and in your name drive out demons and perform many miracles?" Then I will tell them plainly, "I never knew you. Away from me, you evildoers!"

Just because we know of Jesus and we do things in His name doesn't mean we have a relationship with Him. If He doesn't know us, He considers us evildoers and we won't get to heaven. Jesus is saying that it's all about our relationship with him.

Look at what Jesus said about the wise and foolish builders in Matthew 7:24–27.

Therefore everyone who hears these words of mine and puts them into practice is like a wise man who built his house on the rock. The rain came down, the streams rose, and the winds blew and beat against that house; yet it did not fall, because it had its foundation on the rock.

But everyone who hears these words of mine and does not put them into practice is like a foolish man who built his house on sand. The rain came down, the streams rose, and the winds blew and beat against that house, and it fell with a great crash.

Jesus was teaching us that we are to build our lives by putting into practice what He has taught. We need to do what He says, not just be aware of it. What do you think the meaning of Jesus's parable is? Are you putting His words into practice? What does it mean that the foolish man's house fell with a great crash?

Let's look at what Jesus said in Luke 13:24–30.

Make every effort to enter through the narrow door, because many, I tell you, will try to enter and will not be able to. Once the owner of the house gets up and closes the door, you will stand outside knocking and pleading, "Sir, open the door for us." But he will answer, "I don't know you or where you come from."

Then you will say, "We ate and drank with you, and you taught in our streets." But he will reply, "I don't know you or where you come from. Away from me, all you evildoers!"

There will be weeping there, and gnashing of teeth, when you see Abraham, Isaac and Jacob and all the prophets in the kingdom of God, but you yourselves thrown out. People will come from east and west and north and south, and will take their places at the feast in the kingdom of God. Indeed there are those who are last who will be first, and first who will be last.

At your time of judgment with Jesus, when He recaps your life as you kneel in His presence, what will He say to you? Will He say, "Who are you?" or "I don't know you"? I hope not; that would be dreadful. Jesus said those people will go where there is weeping and the gnashing of teeth. I believe that place is hell. Jesus wants a deep, close, and personal relationship with us. He wants to know us, and He wants us to know Him.

If we aren't walking the narrow path after entering through the narrow gate, we're in danger. Jesus said the risk would be high. And just because we're around Jesus doesn't mean we have a relationship with Him—and a relationship is what He wants.

Let's look at a parable in Luke 14:16–24, in which a man (who represents Jesus) is preparing a banquet for His invited guests.

> Jesus replied: "A certain man was preparing a great banquet and invited many guests. At the time of the banquet he sent his servant to tell those who had been invited, 'Come, for everything is now ready.'
>
> But they all alike began to make excuses. The first said, 'I have just bought a field, and I must go and see it. Please excuse me.' Another said, 'I have just bought five yoke of oxen, and I'm on my way to try them out. Please excuse me.' Still another said, 'I just got married, so I can't come.'
>
> The servant came back and reported this to his master. Then the owner of the house became angry and ordered his servant, 'Go out quickly into the streets and alleys of the town and bring in the poor, the crippled, the blind and the lame.'
>
> 'Sir,' the servant said, 'what you ordered has been done, but there is still room.'
>
> Then the master told his servant, 'Go out to the roads and country lanes and make them come in, so that my house will be full. I tell

you, not one of those men who were invited
will get a taste of my banquet.'"

We are invited into a relationship with Jesus, and He
expects us to accept this invitation. If we don't, we will be
denied entrance to the banquet, which I believe will be
served in heaven.

Notice how busy some of the people in the parable
were. Some explained that they had good things to do, like
tending to new oxen or a bride. But notice also that the
master didn't say something like, "Oh, I understand why
you're not coming. What you're doing is good and noble."
The master became angry with these invited guests. You
can almost hear Him saying, "How dare you busy yourself
with anything else besides coming to my banquet?" It seems
that Jesus is asking us to determine what our top priority
is. What are your priorities? Is Jesus the number one? He
wants your relationship with Him to be your top priority.
He doesn't want any excuses.

Pay close attention to Jesus's statements directed at some
Pharisees in John 5:39–44.

> You diligently study the Scriptures because
> you think that by them you possess eternal
> life. These are the Scriptures that testify
> about me, yet you refuse to come to me to
> have life.

> I do not accept praise from men, but I know
> you. I know that you do not have the love
> of God in your hearts. I have come in my
> Father's name, and you do not accept me;

> but if someone else comes in his own name,
> you will accept him.
>
> How can you believe if you accept praise
> from one another, yet make no effort to
> obtain the praise that comes from the
> only God.

Jesus was upset with the Pharisees. They just didn't believe Him. They studied the Scriptures and placed all their faith in them instead of in Jesus, who was standing right there in front of them. They rejected Him. They denied Him! It seems that the Pharisees were keeping their focus on what they knew of the Old Testament and their developed traditions. But Jesus was telling them that their gaze was wrong. Eternal life won't come from just studying and knowing the Scriptures. Eternal life will come only from Jesus. He wants us to believe in Him and develop an intimate relationship with Him.

In John 6:47–58, Jesus speaks about being the bread of life.

> "I tell you the truth, he who believes has
> everlasting life. I am the bread of life. Your
> forefathers ate the manna in the desert, yet
> they died. But here is the bread that comes
> down from heaven, which a man may eat
> and not die.
>
> I am the living bread that came down from
> heaven. If anyone eats of this bread, he will
> live forever. This bread is my flesh, which

I will give for the life of the world." Then the Jews began to argue sharply among themselves, "How can this man give us his flesh to eat?"

Jesus said to them, "I tell you the truth, unless you eat the flesh of the Son of Man and drink his blood, you have no life in you. Whoever eats my flesh and drinks my blood has eternal life, and I will raise him up at the last day. For my flesh is real food and my blood is real drink.

Whoever eats my flesh and drinks my blood remains in me, and I in him. Just as the living Father sent me and I live because of the Father, so the one who feeds on me will live because of me. This is the bread that came down from heaven. Your forefathers ate manna and died, but he who feeds on this bread will live forever."

I can only imagine what it would be like to be a Pharisee or some other Jew and hear Jesus ask me to eat His flesh and drink His blood! What would I have thought Jesus meant? If we eat His flesh and drink His blood, then Jesus will be what fuels us. He will be our food, which we all know is necessary for life. As we eat and drink of Him, He will be present throughout our bodies. Our bodies will assimilate Him, and He will be the life that is in every cell of our being. Jesus was not describing a casual relationship; He was calling us into the most intimate of relationships.

In verse 56, Jesus said, "Whoever eats my flesh and drinks my blood remains in me and I in him." Does this describe this a once-and-done relationship? Do two people get married and then live separate lives? No way! The wedding is just the beginning of the relationship, the beginning of learning to live together and developing a lifelong relationship.

Jesus wants your life. What is the cost of being a disciple? Everything! But what does it mean to give up everything? I believe Jesus was asking us to die to our old earthly, sinful ways and come to life in His ways. Paul described it well in Colossians 3:5–10.

> Put to death, therefore, whatever belongs to your earthly nature: sexual immorality, impurity, lust, evil desires and greed, which is idolatry. Because of these, the wrath of God is coming. You used to walk in these ways, in the life you once lived.

> But now you must also rid yourselves of all such things as these: anger, rage, malice, slander, and filthy language from your lips. Do not lie to each other, since you have taken off your old self with its practices and have put on the new self, which is being renewed in knowledge in the image of its Creator.

Jesus paid the price so we could have a relationship with Him. Are you willing to do your part? Are you willing to give up everything and work at developing a deep, close, and intimate relationship with Him? What would you be willing to do or give up to have such a relationship with Jesus?

Jesus had something to say about that too. Let's look at the parable of the hidden treasure and the pearl in Matthew 13:44–46.

> The kingdom of heaven is like treasure hidden in a field. When a man found it, he hid it again, and then in his joy went and sold all he had and bought that field. Again, the kingdom of heaven is like a merchant looking for fine pearls. When he found one of great value, he went away and sold everything he had and bought it.

What was Jesus teaching us with this parable? When we become aware of and connect with the kingdom of heaven, we're expected to see value in it and set aside everything to gain it. Am I setting everything aside to have this relationship with Jesus? If I'm not, will there be eternal consequences? Will this impact the decision Jesus will make regarding my eternal life with Him?

Luke 10:25-37 is the parable of the good Samaritan. Jesus used it to demonstrate how He wants us to act if we want to have eternal life with Him.

> On one occasion an expert in the law stood up to test Jesus. "Teacher," he asked, "what must I do to inherit eternal life?" "What is written in the Law?" he replied. "How do you read it?"

> He answered: "'Love the Lord your God
> with all your heart and with all your soul
> and with all your strength and with all
> your mind'; and, 'Love your neighbor as
> yourself.'" "You have answered correctly,"
> Jesus replied. "Do this and you will live."

Jesus is saying here that we are to love God with all we have and also to love our neighbor as ourselves; if we do this, we will have eternal life with Him. So who is our neighbor, and how are we supposed to love them? Here is Jesus's answer to these questions:

> But he wanted to justify himself, so he
> asked Jesus, "And who is my neighbor?" In
> reply Jesus said: "A man was going down
> from Jerusalem to Jericho, when he fell into
> the hands of robbers. They stripped him
> of his clothes, beat him and went away,
> leaving him half dead.

> A priest happened to be going down the
> same road, and when he saw the man, he
> passed by on the other side. So too, a Levite,
> when he came to the place and saw him,
> passed by on the other side.

> But a Samaritan, as he traveled, came where
> the man was; and when he saw him, he took
> pity on him. He went to him and bandaged
> his wounds, pouring on oil and wine. Then

he put the man on his own donkey, took him to an inn and took care of him.

The next day he took out two silver coins and gave them to the innkeeper. 'Look after him,' he said, 'and when I return, I will reimburse you for any extra expense you may have.'

Which of these three do you think was a neighbor to the man who fell into the hands of robbers?" The expert in the law replied, "The one who had mercy on him." Jesus told him, "Go and do likewise."

We can learn from this parable that if we want to have eternal life with Jesus, we need to love God with all our heart, mind, body, and soul, *and* love our neighbor as ourselves. Jesus demonstrated how we are to love our neighbor by making a Samaritan something of a hero in His parable. Remember that the Samaritans were a detestable group to the Israelites. Their hatred for the Samaritans was so bad that when the Israelites traveled south out of Jerusalem, they would walk around Samaria to avoid them, adding significant distance to their journeys.

Imagine someone whom you can't stand being around, someone who is detestable in your sight. This is the neighbor Jesus was saying you need to love as you love yourself. The standard is high.

Jesus is not calling us into a casual way of life; He expects us to perform. He knows it will be hard and fraught with many troubles. That said, He didn't leave us to do this alone;

He will help us and guide us. The Holy Spirit is with us and will give us His divine power to perform these great things.

But remember that even though He is here with us, we still have to do the work and put in the effort. I don't believe Jesus is as concerned about the results of our work as much as He is about our intentions and efforts. We're responsible for doing what we're supposed to do, not for the results of these actions—Jesus will handle that. If we're trying to do good, follow Him, and love others, He'll know that we are trying. When we fail, we can repent of our sins and fall back into His grace, mercy, and love.

Do you think Jesus sees a difference between those who try with all their might, yet fail, and those who don't put in a full effort and fail? This will resonate with parents. If children make a great effort to do something good, yet fail, their parents' hearts nonetheless fill with compassion and love because they know how hard their children were trying. Children might make all kinds of messes when they fail, but parents have it in their hearts to look past the messes to see the great effort. On the other hand, parents also know when their children aren't trying hard, or even at all, or when they are intentionally messing up. In such cases, parents might feel frustrated or disappointed, knowing their children know better and could do better.

Understanding this point makes me wonder about Jesus. Does He look on us differently if we're really trying—even if we're failing—as opposed to not trying at all? I think He does. I think He wants us to put our faith into action and follow Him, serve others, and love our neighbor. The Holy Spirit will be right there with us, bringing His divine power into our circumstances.

But what if we're reckless and don't make heartfelt efforts day in and day out? What if we aren't really trying? What if we're not doing what Jesus commanded that we be doing when He returns? Will it have an effect on our going to heaven versus hell? Is the road to heaven really just about a transaction, or is it something else? What basis will Jesus use to evaluate us on our day of judgment? I don't think His judgment will be based solely on whether we did the transaction. I believe there will be more to it.

Review Questions

- What does it mean to have a close, personal, and intimate relationship with Jesus?
- Just because we know of Jesus and, maybe, do some things in His name, does that mean we have a relationship with Him? Why or why not?
- In Luke 14, Jesus taught the parable of the great banquet. It seemed that some people had pretty good excuses for not attending the banquet. One needed to check out some new land, another wanted to tend a new ox, and yet another had a new wife. What was the master's response to the people's excuses? Why do you suppose the master responded this way? How does this parable apply to us today?

CHAPTER 8

The Parables

If you have completed the Bible study of Matthew 24 and 25 in the back of this book, you now get to reap the harvest of all your work. I hope you've been considering what Jesus said in these two chapters and what He meant when He taught the three parables. But for those who haven't yet done the study, I'll try to give plenty of context so you can see what's going on.

In this chapter, we'll read through most of Matthew 24 and 25. I will try to unpack it in sections. These two chapters in Matthew are one continuous discussion between Jesus and His disciples, not a piecemeal summary of different conversations. Jesus had an important message to leave us, and He gave it plenty of attention here. He told us what the end times will be like, comparing them to the times of Noah. Then he told a number of parables that describe how we should live if we consider ourselves His disciples. Though we may not like to hear it, Jesus told us what His judgment of us will be if we choose not to live the way He asked us to.

In this part of the book of Matthew, Jesus was nearing the end of His earthly life and was about to be betrayed by Judas. In chapter 23, Jesus finished teaching in the temple in Jerusalem. The Pharisees were challenging Him, and He really let them have it. He called them blind guides and told them about their seven woes. He said the Pharisees appeared righteous to people, but on the inside, they were full of hypocrisy and wickedness. After this intense interaction, Jesus left the temple. We pick up the action in Matthew 24.

> Jesus left the temple and was walking away when his disciples came up to him to call his attention to its buildings. "Do you see all these things?" he asked. "I tell you the truth, not one stone here will be left on another; every one will be thrown down."

> As Jesus was sitting on the Mount of Olives, the disciples came to him privately. "Tell us," they said, "when will this happen, and what will be the sign of your coming and of the end of the age?"

> Jesus answered: "Watch out that no one deceives you. For many will come in my name, claiming, 'I am the Christ,' and will deceive many. You will hear of wars and rumors of wars, but see to it that you are not alarmed. Such things must happen, but the end is still to come.

Nation will rise against nation, and kingdom against kingdom. There will be famines and earthquakes in various places. All these are the beginning of birth pains.

Then you will be handed over to be persecuted and put to death, and you will be hated by all nations because of me. At that time many will turn away from the faith and will betray and hate each other, and many false prophets will appear and deceive many people.

Because of the increase of wickedness, the love of most will grow cold, but he who stands firm to the end will be saved. And this gospel of the kingdom will be preached in the whole world as a testimony to all nations, and then the end will come."

Jesus said that the end of the age will be a terrible time: nation against nation, kingdom against kingdom. In verse 10, He said many will turn away from their faith in Him. In verse 12, He said the love of most people will grow cold. Since Jesus is love and these people will turn away from their faith, it makes sense that their love will grow cold. Notice that in verse 13 he spoke of those who would be saved. He did not say those who have once professed a faith in Him or those who have done the transaction will be saved; He said that those who stand firm in their faith until the end will be saved.

In verse 36, He described how the day and the hour of the end times are unknown.

> No one knows about that day or hour, not even the angels in heaven, nor the Son, but only the Father. As it was in the days of Noah, so it will be at the coming of the Son of Man. For in the days before the flood, people were eating and drinking, marrying and giving in marriage, up to the day Noah entered the ark; and they knew nothing about what would happen until the flood came and took them all away. That is how it will be at the coming of the Son of Man.

> Two men will be in the field; one will be taken and the other left. Two women will be grinding with a hand mill; one will be taken and the other left. Therefore keep watch, because you do not know on what day your Lord will come.

> But understand this: If the owner of the house had known at what time of night the thief was coming, he would have kept watch and would not have let his house be broken into. So you also must be ready, because the Son of Man will come at an hour when you do not expect him.

Jesus asked us to be ready. What does that mean? How does one prepare for Jesus's return? I think it means that we should live completely dependent on Jesus; we should set our lives aside and live for Him. We should allow the Holy Spirit to reign in our hearts and have His way with us.

Back in the days of Noah, did the people have God at the center of their lives? I don't think so. Jesus said they were just going about their day-to-day activities. Does this sound familiar to you? They were eating, drinking, marrying—and then it was too late. Maybe they should have been doing God's business instead of their own. He said that the consequences of not keeping watch are being swept away or left behind.

Then Jesus thoughtfully told a story to teach about being ready. The master of a house went away for a long time, leaving his servant in charge of many things.

> Who then is the faithful and wise servant, whom the master has put in charge of the servants in his household to give them their food at the proper time? It will be good for that servant whose master finds him doing so when he returns. I tell you the truth, he will put him in charge of all his possessions.
>
> But suppose that servant is wicked and says to himself, "My master is staying away a long time," and he then begins to beat his fellow servants and to eat and drink with drunkards. The master of that servant will come on a day when he does not expect him and at an hour he is not aware of.

He will cut him to pieces and assign him a
place with the hypocrites, where there will
be weeping and gnashing of teeth.

Jesus told us this story to help us understand how He wants us to live. He said that He would go away for a long time. Today, Jesus has been away for over two thousand years. He also said that He expected us to act and live appropriately while He was gone, by loving God with all our heart, mind, and soul, and loving others. Jesus wants us to make the effort, develop our relationship with Him, and do His business.

Notice what Jesus said will happen if He comes back and finds we aren't acting the way He wants us to: "He will cut him to pieces and assign him a place with the hypocrites where there will be weeping and gnashing of teeth." That's hell.

Who goes to heaven and who goes to hell? That will be up to Jesus. He's been given full authority by God to judge us. But the bigger question is, what will He base this decision on? Will it depend on our having done a transaction to receive the Holy Spirit, or on our having a lifelong, deep, close, and personal relationship with Him?

Jesus was clear in this section of Scripture. He expects us to live the way He showed us and to follow His ways. He also told us about the consequences of not living this way. Because, I think, He really wanted us to get this point, He continued this discussion with His disciples by sharing three parables in Matthew 25. The parable of the ten virgins is the first of the three.

At that time the kingdom of heaven will be like ten virgins who took their lamps and went out to meet the bridegroom. Five of them were foolish and five were wise. The foolish ones took their lamps but did not take any oil with them. The wise, however, took oil in jars along with their lamps.

The bridegroom was a long time in coming, and they all became drowsy and fell asleep. At midnight the cry rang out: "Here's the bridegroom! Come out to meet him!" Then all the virgins woke up and trimmed their lamps.

The foolish ones said to the wise, "Give us some of your oil; our lamps are going out." "No," they replied, "there may not be enough for both us and you. Instead, go to those who sell oil and buy some for yourselves."

But while they were on their way to buy the oil, the bridegroom arrived. The virgins who were ready went in with him to the wedding banquet. And the door was shut. Later the others also came. "Sir! Sir!" they said. "Open the door for us!"

But he replied, "I tell you the truth, I don't know you." Therefore keep watch, because you do not know the day or the hour.

In this parable, the virgins represent believers. Why else would they be waiting for the return of the bridegroom, Jesus? The wise virgins were those who lived in readiness, waiting for Jesus's return.

What does it mean to live in readiness? If you attend church, are you ready? If you take part in a Bible study group, are you ready? Maybe, maybe not. What do you think? What will the consequences be if you aren't ready or living the way Jesus showed you? When you knock on the door of heaven, will Jesus say He doesn't know you? Will the door to heaven swing shut? Jesus will deny entrance to those didn't live their lives in readiness.

If you were to honestly evaluate your life, would you say you were living in readiness? Maybe the other question to ponder is this: Does it matter?

Let's continue with the parable of the talents.

> Again, it will be like a man going on a journey, who called his servants and entrusted his property to them. To one he gave five talents of money, to another two talents, and to another one talent, each according to his ability. Then he went on his journey. The man who had received the five talents went at once and put his money to work and gained five more. So also, the one with the two talents gained two more. But the man who had received the one talent went off, dug a hole in the ground and hid his master's money.

After a long time the master of those servants returned and settled accounts with them. The man who had received the five talents brought the other five. "Master," he said, "you entrusted me with five talents. See, I have gained five more."

His master replied, "Well done, good and faithful servant! You have been faithful with a few things; I will put you in charge of many things. Come and share your master's happiness!"

The man with the two talents also came. "Master," he said, "you entrusted me with two talents; see, I have gained two more."

His master replied, "Well done, good and faithful servant! You have been faithful with a few things; I will put you in charge of many things. Come and share your master's happiness!"

Then the man who had received the one talent came. "Master," he said, "I knew that you are a hard man, harvesting where you have not sown and gathering where you have not scattered seed. So I was afraid and went out and hid your talent in the ground. See, here is what belongs to you."

His master replied, "You wicked, lazy servant! So you knew that I harvest where I have not sown and gather where I have not scattered seed? Well then, you should have put my money on deposit with the bankers, so that when I returned I would have received it back with interest.

Take the talent from him and give it to the one who has the ten talents. For everyone who has will be given more, and he will have an abundance. Whoever does not have, even what he has will be taken from him. And throw that worthless servant outside, into the darkness, where there will be weeping and gnashing of teeth."

Jesus was turning up the heat in this parable. The servants in this parable represent believers, and the master represents Jesus. Jesus gave all His believers gifts, talents, and the Holy Spirit. Jesus expected that while he was away—as He is now—His gifts would be used to further His kingdom. He gave more talents to some than to others. Some put their God-given talents to work and furthered His kingdom, but the last servant did nothing with his God-given talent except bury it so others couldn't benefit from it. To put it another way, he did the transaction and received the Holy Spirit, but didn't live his life following Jesus. As a result, the master ordered, "Throw that worthless servant outside, into the darkness, where there will be weeping and gnashing of teeth." I believe Jesus was saying that if you aren't using your God-given talents to further His kingdom, to hell you go.

Jesus kept the discussion going with this third parable. He must have thought this point was extremely important and wanted us to get it, as He used the parables to give three different perspectives on the same subject. If the first two parables aren't clear enough, maybe this one about the sheep and the goats will be.

> When the Son of Man comes in his glory, and all the angels with him, he will sit on his throne in heavenly glory. All the nations will be gathered before him, and he will separate the people one from another as a shepherd separates the sheep from the goats. He will put the sheep on his right and the goats on his left.
>
> Then the King will say to those on his right, "Come, you who are blessed by my Father; take your inheritance, the kingdom prepared for you since the creation of the world. For I was hungry and you gave me something to eat, I was thirsty and you gave me something to drink, I was a stranger and you invited me in, I needed clothes and you clothed me, I was sick and you looked after me, I was in prison and you came to visit me."
>
> Then the righteous will answer him, "Lord, when did we see you hungry and feed you,

or thirsty and give you something to drink? When did we see you a stranger and invite you in, or needing clothes and clothe you? When did we see you sick or in prison and go to visit you?"

The King will reply, "I tell you the truth, whatever you did for one of the least of these brothers of mine, you did for me." Then he will say to those on his left, "Depart from me, you who are cursed, into the eternal fire prepared for the devil and his angels.

For I was hungry and you gave me nothing to eat, I was thirsty and you gave me nothing to drink, I was a stranger and you did not invite me in, I needed clothes and you did not clothe me, I was sick and in prison and you did not look after me."

They also will answer, "Lord, when did we see you hungry or thirsty or a stranger or needing clothes or sick or in prison, and did not help you?"

He will reply, "I tell you the truth, whatever you did not do for one of the least of these, you did not do for me. Then they will go away to eternal punishment, but the righteous to eternal life."

Jesus was telling us that when the end times come, He will judge us and separate us based on that judgment. The sheep represent the righteous; they will live for eternity with Jesus in heaven. But others, represented by the goats, will spend eternity in hell.

In the parable, what was Jesus's basis for judgment? Let me point out first what it wasn't: He didn't say His judgment would be based on whether or not we have done the transaction. Jesus's judgment in the parable was based on whether people had served others and, while doing so, developed their relationship with Him. Those who didn't serve Jesus by serving others clearly didn't have a relationship with Him. The consequence of their lack of faith in action would be eternal punishment.

Some people have challenged me about my understanding of Jesus's teachings in relation to His judgment of us. Many of them tell me that what we do does not affect Jesus's judgment for our salvation, because that would be *earning our way to heaven*. They say it will be all about what Jesus did, He did everything, we do nothing; after we have completed the transaction, what we do will have no impact on His judgment of our eternal life. Please allow me to point out something very important that might help clear the air on this topic. Within chapters 24 and 25 in Matthew, Jesus used four parables to teach us about the basis he will use when He judges those who go to heaven and those who go to hell.

In the first parable, the master went away for a long time and the servant who did not do what he was supposed to be doing was assigned to hell. In this parable, Jesus is the master and we are the servant. When the servant was judged to go to hell, was it based on what the master did, or on what the servant did? We know for sure that it was based on what the servant did, because he beat his fellow servants and ate and drank with the drunkards.

What about the parable of the virgins? Five of the virgins were denied entrance into a banquet, which represents heaven. Was this denial based on what they did or did not do or was it based on what bridegroom did or did not do? They were denied heaven because they had not been ready when the bridegroom came.

In the parable of the talents, one of the servants was thrown into hell. Was that judgment based on what the master did or did not do? No, it was based on what the servant did. The servant buried the talent and did nothing else with it.

Last is the parable of the sheep and the goats. The sheep will be considered righteous and spend eternity in heaven, but the goats will spend eternity in the eternal fire prepared for the devil and his angels. The judgment was based not on what the Son of Man did, but on what the people did or did not do. Those who fed the hungry, gave the thirsty something to drink, and clothed the needy were considered sheep. I hope you see the point Jesus was making with these four parables. He is clear: we play a role in how we will be judged.

So how do we wrap up these two heavy chapters in Matthew? Jesus knew He would be away for a while. Only the Father knows how long. But when He comes back, He will expect His followers to have been putting their faith into action and advancing His kingdom. We need to guard against letting our faith grow cold and we must stand firm to the end. We need to be about Jesus's business, keep watch, be ready like the five wise virgins, use our God-given talents to further God's kingdom, and serve Jesus by serving others.

Please remember this important point. Salvation is not about executing certain tasks and hoping, thereby, that we have gained salvation; that is called working your way to heaven and it doesn't work. Instead, it is all about being transformed by the power of the Holy Spirit. It's about being alive in your heart. When you have His life in you, you'll be doing the kinds of things that Jesus taught in these parables because the Holy Spirit will be leading you; that will be the natural outflow of God alive in your heart. The reward will be eternity with our Lord and Savior. But the punishment for not doing so will be eternity with Satan in hell. I hope you notice the difference I am trying to make. Having a relationship with Jesus is not just about completing tasks on a list. It is about having the Holy Spirit alive in you; what you then do is a natural outflow of His presence working within you.

It is indescribably good to repent and turn away from a life of sin, turn to Jesus, accept Him as our Lord and Savior, and receive Him and His gift of the Holy Spirit. Jesus called this being born again. This transaction is a complete transformation of the soul. It is a beautiful beginning, but only that—a beginning. Jesus now expects us to put these talents into play to further His kingdom. Choosing not to do so with all our heart, mind, body, and soul could have eternal consequences. That is something I do not want to risk. How about you?

Review Questions

- In Matthew 24:46, Jesus said it would be good for the servant to be doing what he was supposed to be doing when the master returned. What happened to the servant when he chose not to do what was asked of him? How does this apply to us today?
- In the parable of the virgins, five of them were denied entrance into heaven. Why do you think they were denied? How does this apply to us today?
- In the parable of the talents, one servant was thrown into hell. Why do you think he was punished this way? How does this apply to us today?
- In the parable of the sheep and the goats, the goats are separated out and sent to hell. Why is this? How does this apply to us today?
- Are you ready for Jesus's return?

CHAPTER 9

The Stadium

As you know by now, I love analogies and stories. They help me see things from a different perspective. Here's an analogy that helped me understand what Jesus wants of me. It relates to a football game and a stadium.

There are essentially three types of people in this story. The first type is those who don't care whether or not there's a football game going on. They don't come to the stadium; they may not even know there's a game on. They go about their day as if it were any other. They couldn't care less about the game.

The second type is those who come to the game and sit in the stands. Some people call them fans; they really care about the game. They're much closer to the action than those who don't come, but they're content to just watch.

The third type is the players. They love the game, just as those in the stands do, but they love it so much that they take the field. They're not content with just watching; they want to play. They're part of a team and develop camaraderie and intimacy with one another by playing—something those in the stands cannot do.

Those on the field have great memories and can share many stories about the experience of being in the game, where they experience pains, soreness, defeats, wins, and touchdowns; they share in the joy of it all with their teammates. They have a special relationship with each other by virtue of being on the team.

Perhaps one player breaks a finger during a play. He shares this with a teammate—not because he's complaining, but because he needs help. His teammate responds, "Don't worry, I've got your back." These kinds of situations develop intimacy and deep relationships.

There's a sense of vulnerability on the field that allows them to play and enjoy the game and enter deep, meaningful relationships with other players. Furthermore, these kind of relationships can be developed only by playing the game and being on the field. Those who have been on teams like this will understand the principle.

So how does this analogy relate to our spiritual walk? Let's look a little more closely at the three groups of people. Those who don't come to the game are those who have heard the good news about Jesus, but don't believe in Him. They don't want Jesus in their lives and are content with life on their own terms. I don't know all the reasons they might have for not believing; let's just say they're not believers. The Bible is clear regarding the eternal life of nonbelievers. They will live for eternity in hell, not with Jesus in heaven. I don't mean to be harsh in saying this, but I didn't create this story or the rules. These people will have their moment when they meet Jesus—then they'll know the truth. The bummer is that it will be too late for them. During their earthly lives, though, they could have chosen differently. These people are the lost sheep Jesus commanded us to reach and to share His good news with! Jesus is counting on us to reach them with the gospel story. So let's keep praying for these people and bringing them His good news.

Who are the fans in this analogy? Clearly, they are people who are interested in Jesus—otherwise, why would they come to the game? They love to see others enjoying a deep relationship with Jesus, and maybe they wonder in some strange way whether they have what it takes to have a relationship with Him. Maybe they think they're not worthy. Maybe they think that since they attend church services and pay attention to the pastor, they have a "good enough" relationship with Jesus. Maybe they've done some terrible things and somehow think that Jesus wouldn't or couldn't love them or desire a relationship with them. I don't know all their reasons, but still, something in their hearts draws them close. Nonetheless, they have trouble making the decision to follow Jesus and have a close, deep, and intimate relationship with Him.

Maybe they're afraid of not being in control of their lives. Maybe they're afraid of what they might become or that Jesus might ask them to change certain behaviors. Maybe they fear the unknown. *What would it be like on the field?* they may wonder. Maybe they have fears of getting hurt or not being able to play well or being made fun of. Maybe they enjoy being fans and consider that to be enough; after all, it's safe. Maybe they were taught in church that this was all they needed to do. There's little risk in sitting in the stands, where they can cheer on or jeer at those on the field. They can come and go as they please and stay as close to the game as they choose. No coach tells them what to do or holds them accountable. Maybe they chose to follow Jesus because they thought He would give them a good earthly life with much pleasure and prosperity. You could say that they enjoy being warmed by the fire; they know they're close to something that's good, but they will come no closer.

But I don't think Jesus is asking us simply to come and be warmed by the fire. I believe He's asking us to jump into it. No matter what their reasoning, these people probably consider themselves Christians, have done the transaction and received the Holy Spirit, go to church, maybe attend a Bible study, pray before meals, give money to the needy, and are basically good people. I don't know all the Christian activities they may do. But if they're in the stands, I know that they don't live a life committed to Jesus, aren't developing a deep and intimate relationship with Jesus, aren't trying to keep Him as their number-one priority, nor are they putting much effort into living as students and followers of their Lord and Savior, Jesus Christ.

They may feel that they could play on the field someday, but not today. Maybe they think they're not quite ready for this change. Look at what they were taught: from a standpoint of eternal life, there is nothing at stake, so what's the risk in staying in the stands? They've done the transaction, so they believe they're saved and will live eternally with Jesus. That's what they were taught. That's what they believe.

But what if they are wrong? What if the leaders of our Christian churches are mistaken? What would that mean for the people in the stands? What if their eternal lives depend on getting out there on the field? How tragic would it be, then, if they didn't?

I'm not accusing our church leaders of knowingly and intentionally leading us astray, but I am saying they're mistaken. What if this is one of Satan's greatest deceptions of all time? Is this possible? You've been reading what Jesus had to say about the entrance into heaven. Are you going to listen to the church leaders or Jesus? If you think you're in the stands, my hope is that you quickly change things and make your way to the playing field!

Now let's talk about the people on the field. They are trying to develop a deep, personal, and intimate relationship with Jesus, making Him their number one priority, and making a meaningful and heartfelt attempt to include Jesus in all they are and do. Just like those in the stands, they've done the transaction and received the Holy Spirit, they go to church, maybe attend a Bible study, pray before meals, give money to the needy, and are basically good people. But there's something more going on in them than in those in the stands: they have a desire to be in a relationship with Jesus and to make the effort to maintain a deep, close, and intimate relationship with Him. They try to humbly walk with Jesus day and night.

In his daily devotional, *My Utmost For His Highest* (December 18), Oswald Chambers spoke about our relationship with Jesus.

> Being faithful to Jesus Christ is the most difficult thing we try to do today. We will be faithful to our work, to serving others,

or to anything else; just don't ask us to be faithful to Jesus Christ. Many Christians become very impatient when we talk about faithfulness to Jesus. Our Lord is dethroned more deliberately by Christian workers than by the world. We treat God as if He were a machine designed to bless us, and we think of Jesus as just another one of the workers.

The goal of faithfulness is not that we will do work for God, but that He will be free to do His work through us. God calls us to His service and places tremendous responsibilities on us. He expects no complaining on our parts and offers no explanation on His part. God wants to use us as He used His own Son.

What Chambers is saying here is that our faithful walk with Jesus will be tough. In our Christian walk, we should not be content only with faithfully doing service work. We are to be faithful to Jesus. As the Holy Spirit comes alive within us, He will tell us how we are to serve; it will be a natural outflowing of our heart. The question Mr. Chambers drives home is: Will we allow God to do His work through us? Jesus is saying that He wants us to be in constant contact with Him, continuously walking with Him on the path. He wants us to be living with Him and always aware of His presence. Our relationship with Jesus is to be the focus and center of all we are and do. He's not asking us to make our spouse, our career, our children, or our activities number one. Nor is he asking us to make football, baseball, hockey, car racing, hunting, fishing, or any other sport our number one. He wants our relationship with Him to be our number one priority.

This opened up a few questions for me: *Can I really do this? Is it possible?* The answer is a resounding yes. It is possible to do this, but not by ourselves. We can only do it with the divine power of the Holy Spirit. Once we receive the Holy Spirit, we have to be very intentional with the direction of our lives because God gave us the free will to choose to follow Him. We must desire this relationship with Jesus. If we've done the transaction and received the Holy Spirit, then we're born again. This desire to intimately walk with Jesus is already deep in our hearts because God put it there. Now we have to feed this desire with real, intentional actions.

If this is how you live your life, then you will think about and consider Jesus in all the normal activities of your day; you will be aware of Him as if He were there with you in the flesh. You will think of Him while your head is on your pillow, when you chose what you want for breakfast or what to wear that day, when you are doing activities and making decisions—all the time. He'll be with you when you drive around, and you'll acknowledge His presence with you everywhere you go. You will try to act as He showed you to act, and you will love others as He showed you how to love. You will be His lamp, and He will shine through you.

I have been trying to live this way for over fourteen years now, and I must admit it's not very easy. I fail in some way every day, and on some days, I fail miserably. But the most important thing is not whether or not I'm good at it; what matters is the desires of my heart, my effort, and what I'm trying to do. When I have a bad day, I go to bed, ask for forgiveness, and then sleep. When I wake up, I thank God for a new opportunity to serve Him, and once again, I commit another day to Him. I try to not let yesterday's failures prevent me from trying today, with all my heart, mind, and soul. I try to keep the attitude that today is a new day He created for me. What's most important are my attitude and my intentions; I try to keep them focused on Jesus.

Jesus knows we will have troubles; He knows the troubles we're in right now. He looks at our heart, our intentions, and what we're attempting to do. He knows when we are truly trying to do something, even if we fail. I'm certain He can tell also if we're not trying very hard (or not at all) before we fail. Jesus looks at our true hearts and knows our intentions. He's not as concerned with the results of our actions as He is with our intentions. We're responsible for our attitudes, intentions, and efforts, but not necessarily the results. We can rest, be at ease, and leave the results up to Jesus.

What happens if we don't try? What happens if we remain fans in the seats, never stepping onto the field? Or, as Jesus put it in John 15:5–6, what happens if we don't stay connected to Him, the true vine? Jesus said we'd be like branches that are thrown away, wither, and end up being burned. What do you think He meant? I don't think it's something pleasant.

Today, many Christian churches teach that after you have done the transaction, whether or not you stay connected to Jesus has no impact on where you'll spend eternity. They say this because they believe your eternal salvation was decided when you did the transaction, received Jesus as your Lord and Savior, and received the Holy Spirit. Because of this, many people believe that all they need do is just be around Jesus and know about Him; they have done the transaction and already know they're going to heaven. Some people tell me that they did the transaction and know they are going to heaven—but that when they get to heaven they may only get the garden apartment versus the penthouse. They say this because they know they do not try to follow Jesus or try to make Him a priority in their lives. In other words, they are saying that what they do after the transaction only builds up rewards they will receive when they get to heaven and has nothing to do with their eternal salvation. I disagree with this view, but many churches teach this view of Christianity. I believe it's inconsistent with the Bible and is not at all what Jesus taught us.

Some people say, "I'm a work in progress," or "I'm not ready to give up my worldly wealth and comfort just to have a better place in heaven," or "It's just not worth it; I'm headed to heaven anyway, so why do I really have to try?"

Sometimes, they compare their behavior to that of other Christians and say things like, "These people call themselves Christians and look what they do," or "If they're Christians and they do that, then so can I." Because their self-comparison doesn't reveal any significant differences, they think everything must be okay. But consider this: Is that really the comparison we are supposed to be making? Shouldn't we be comparing ourselves to the Bible?

Compare the statistics of Christians who attend church to those good and moral nonbelievers. The divorce rate in both groups is the same, as are the rates of abortion and addiction the same. Both groups listen to much of the same music and do the same activities. How can this be? Jesus said that if we followed Him, we'd look radically different from non-Christians. But that's not the case today. Something is wrong in today's church.

How many people watch movies or do other things detestable to God and then come to church professing to be a Christian? How many churchgoing Christians closely follow and cheer for movie stars and pro athletes who act in ways revolting to God? I'm not referring to people who unintentionally fall into occasional sin, but to people who knowingly make such ways their lifestyle.

If we are Christians who follow Jesus, then we will be new creations and we will not conform to the world. We will be transformed by the power of the Holy Spirit dwelling in our hearts. We will die to sin in our lives and choose things that glorify God.

Jesus didn't call us to follow Him and just be good; He called us to be holy and to be His. God is a holy God. If we are Christians who follow His Son, then we should clearly manifest this. We should not look like the rest of the world; we should stand out and look different.

The statistics say that most people in America claim to be Christian, but that's because they did the transaction once upon a time and someone told them that made them a Christian, regardless of what they did after. But this is not necessarily so. Let's look at James 2:14–19.

> What good is it, my brothers and sisters,
> if someone claims to have faith but has no

deeds? Can such faith save them? Suppose a brother or a sister is without clothes and daily food. If one of you says to them, "Go in peace; keep warm and well fed," but does nothing about their physical needs, what good is it? In the same way, faith by itself, if it is not accompanied by action, is dead.

But someone will say, "You have faith; I have deeds." Show me your faith without deeds, and I will show you my faith by my deeds. You believe that there is one God. Good! Even the demons believe that—and shudder.

James was saying that those who have faith in Jesus should be doing good deeds. Without deeds, faith is dead. If you're a Christian, you will act like one. Jesus will be the theme of your life. He will be your main focus, and His way of life will be your way of life. If this is not the case, then maybe you don't have faith in Jesus and aren't following Him.

So many Americans, when they accept the responsibility to follow Jesus, believe that it will mean a good earthly life filled with blessings and material things. But Jesus didn't guarantee that at all; in fact, He guaranteed that following Him would be challenging and full of trouble. Jesus didn't even guarantee that our basic needs of food and shelter would be met. Look at John 16:33: "I have told you these things, so that in me you may have peace. In this world you will have trouble. But take heart! I have overcome the world." So why do we now believe so differently from what is stated in the Bible?

Remember the young man who wanted to follow Jesus, but first had to bury his father? Jesus told him to let the dead bury the dead, because there were more important things to be done.

Ask yourself, *Am I trying? Is it my deepest desire to have a personal and intimate relationship with Jesus?* Going back to the stadium story, which type of person are you? Hopefully, you're on the field. But if you're in the stands, ask yourself, *Does it matter?* If you have accepted Jesus as your Lord and Savior, repented of your sins, said the sinner's prayer with a pure and sincere heart, and received Jesus and the Holy Spirit, then does it matter whether you live the way Jesus commanded?

I'm not asking whether you're walking perfectly with Jesus, but whether you're trying to do so with all your heart, mind, body, and soul. In regards to eternal life, if you're not making a sincere effort, does it matter?

What does Jesus say? Does He say that it matters?

Review Questions

- How would you describe the difference between someone who is a fan and someone who is on the field?
- How do you differentiate between doing service work while following and being with Jesus and just doing service work?

- Why do you think the statistics for divorce and drug, alcohol, and sex additions are the same in believers and nonbelievers?
- Is Jesus your number one priority? If not, what is stopping you from making Him number one? Does it matter whether you do or not? Why?

CHAPTER 10

Differences

Now let's spend a little time talking about the difference between someone who has done the transaction, but slowly faded away from Jesus, and someone who has done the transaction and has a close, deep, and intimate relationship with Jesus.

In this chapter, I do not offer biblical truth so much as opinions. Some of what I say will resonate with you and your heart, but some may not. Try to focus on the points that are relevant and meaningful to you and to ignore those that aren't.

Let's start off by defining what a relationship is not. It is not a list of things to do so that, once you've accomplished them, you're in a relationship. Relationships flow from the heart, not from a list. Some people ask, How much do I have to show my wife that I love her before she knows it? What do I have to do to show my wife I love her? I believe these are the wrong questions to be asking. Instead, you may ask yourself questions such as these: How does my wife perceive love? What is my wife's love language? Am I willing to change so I can do the kinds of things she needs from me? Am I willing to do these things out of love for my wife?

What I'm getting at is that we have to look deeper in our hearts and consider what we're trying to do and why. Words such as *intention*, *purpose*, *effort*, and *desire* come to my mind when I think about evaluating the depth and quality of a love relationship.

Relationships are hard to get our arms around. They are complex, multifaceted, and unique because God made each one of us completely different. Not only are men different from women, individuals are different from each other. So when you're thinking about your relationship with Jesus, remember that it's not about the things you do or how many times you do them; doing things and completing tasks do not define a relationship.

You need to look beyond the tasks and try to see why you are doing them. What is motivating you? Why do you do what you do? Many people refer to our relationship with Jesus as living by faith or living by following the Spirit. Our faith in Jesus Christ and our relationship with Him is ever so critical.

Remember: if you have done the transaction, you have the Holy Spirit living in you. You'll be a new creation, transformed from the inside. The good things you do should be things that you want to do, they are the desires of your heart.

When you think about your relationship with Jesus and try to discern whether yours is a casual relationship or an intimate love relationship, what kinds of thoughts come to your mind? How do you even begin to discern the depth or quality of your relationship with Jesus?

Let's start with God's Word in the Bible. Do you desire to be in the Word? I'm asking not if you're in a Bible study, but if you desire to be in the Word in such a way that you just can't get enough of it—like your spirit is hungry and can't get its fill. His Word, the Bible, is alive and is food for the Holy Spirit inside you. Reading the Bible feeds the Spirit. So consider how much you desire to be in the Word. This could be an indicator of the depth of your relationship with Jesus.

Do you have a desire in your heart to deny yourself the luxuries of life so that you might have more to give others, who have nothing? Do you generously give to the poor and the impoverished? Do you give with a joyful heart? Have you chosen a significantly lower standard of living than you can afford so that you might have more to give? Do you give out of your wealth or out of your poverty? I believe that if you are in a deep relationship with Jesus, you will have a desire in your heart to give joyfully and generously. So consider your giving.

Look at your career. Do you feel that God has placed you in your current job? Or is your job merely what needs to be done so you can afford what you have financially committed yourself to and provide for your family? Look at the way you spend time outside of work. What fills your day? Do you believe you're doing things that honor God?

Do you view all your material possessions as objects you're willing to part with? Do you find yourself holding on to some worldly things more than you do spiritual things? For example, do you have a favorite boat that you couldn't do without? Do you continuously fill your mind with ways to remodel or decorate your home? Maybe your car captures your heart. Maybe your closet is filled with special clothes or camping and fishing gear. Could you give these things up? If Jesus asked you to give them up, would you? When you look at your life, do you see your focus more on worldly things or heavenly things? These are possible indicators of the depth of your relationship. Only you and Jesus know the depth of it.

Do you see the material things you have as gifts from God? Try to remember a time when someone loaned you something valuable, like a cabin or a car. Do you remember feeling absolutely wonderful that this person would trust you with this valuable item? Do you remember trying to think about the many ways you could say thank you? Maybe you even wanted to do something special in return for that person. Compare these memories to how you feel about your home or other material items. Do you see them as gifts from God and feel the same way that you did when your friend loaned you something? If not, why? This could be an indicator of the depth of your relationship with Jesus.

Someone once asked me, "What if the things you have tomorrow are only the things you thanked God for today? Then how many things would you have tomorrow?" I thought that was a great question to ponder.

How is your prayer life? Are you in constant contact with the Holy Spirit, or do you pray only before meals and at church? Prayer is one way we connect and communicate with God. Jesus prayed all the time; it was an ordinary part of His everyday life. It was as natural to Him as breathing. Jesus taught us how to pray and gave us the Lord's Prayer.

Let's look at what Paul said in 1 Thessalonians 5:16–18: "Rejoice always, pray continually, give thanks in all circumstances; for this is God's will for you in Christ Jesus." Paul is describing a lifestyle of rejoicing, prayer, and giving thanks. Prayer is not meant to be a part-time activity, but a lifelong one. Do you find yourself praying all the time, in all circumstances, for all people? If that isn't the case, then maybe you should ask yourself why? Does it matter?

When you have faith, live by faith, and follow the Holy Spirit, your heart's desire will be to follow Jesus. You will act more like Him. Your behavior will change. You will be transformed. This process of change can take some time—some might say a lifetime—but the deep desires within your heart will not change, because they come from God. God does not change, nor does His Spirit. Maybe you have layers and years of poor behavior, sin, and disobedience covering your heart. I believe the process of transformation and sanctification is the pruning and removal of the layers of our old, sinful nature that have been accumulated.

Take a moment right now to be with God. Silence yourself and feel the desires of your heart. What do you feel? What do you hear? What do you sense?

Maybe you have never considered these questions before. If that is the case, take a few minutes right now and pause. Feel the desires of your heart. Pray this prayer from Psalm 139:23: "Search me oh God and know my heart: Test me and know my anxious thoughts." When the desires of your heart well up in you, what are they? Are you filled with the desires of Jesus?

Here are a few of the desires of Jesus:

- to be one with the Father
- to love others well
- to live as a living sacrifice
- to live as a servant of all
- to pray
- to be in the word and feed the Spirit
- to feed those who hunger
- to clothe those without

As you consider the above, remember that this is not a checklist of things you should be doing to signify that you're in a deep relationship with Jesus. If you have faith and follow Jesus, then you will want to do these things. They will be your overwhelming heart's desire; they will drive your behavior. Think of the list more as a barometer, a possible indicator of whether you have faith and a deep, close, and intimate relationship with Jesus.

Let's address a new topic: peace. What's the source of your peace? When are you at peace? When are you calm and free of worry or anxiety? As you consider your sense of peace and calm, I want to share a short story with you about a painting contest. Artists were to paint pictures that symbolized peace. The artists could paint anything they wanted, but the pictures had to depict peace. Many wonderful paintings were submitted, but let's talk about the two finalists.

The first finalist's painting was a beautiful landscape. There were majestic, towering, snow-covered mountains in the background. A log cabin was in front and there was a fire burning in the fireplace; you could see the smoke spiraling out of the chimney. There were wildflowers everywhere. You could even see a deer lapping water from a nearby stream. Just one look at this picture and you could sense peace. Who wouldn't feel it in this setting? But this painting didn't win the contest; it came in second place.

The winning painting depicted a violent storm. It was gray and dark. As you looked at the painting, you could hear the wind whistling and feel the torrential rain hitting your face. Leaves were blowing everywhere. In the background was a large rock wall. Tucked into a cleft of a rock on the wall was a mother bird sitting on her nest, in perfect peace.

How could a picture with so much natural violence be a picture of peace? Well, the peace depicted had nothing to do with the storm (the external circumstances), but with the perfect peace of the mother bird sitting on her nest amidst the storm. What picture of peace are you seeking in your life?

I used to seek the peace of the landscape picture. I thought my life would be peaceful when certain circumstances lined up the way I thought they should. But I never achieved this picture of peace. Something would always disturb the picture or get in the way, or someone would do something to interrupt it. My idea of peace was all about me; I knew best how things should be done. I believed I would be at peace if my boss would ran things the way I thought they should be run. I would be at peace if my neighbor would be quiet at night, or if my kids would behave. I would be at peace if I were left alone to have some quiet time. This list would go on forever. I was almost never at peace because my life was never the way I thought it should be.

There were times in my life when I did achieve certain goals, and some things lined up just the way I wanted them. But you know what? I still wasn't content. Either the satisfaction was only temporary, or it did not feel quite like I thought it would. I always wanted something more, something different. I was never really at peace, down deep in my heart.

Then it occurred to me that maybe my life wasn't supposed to look the way I wanted it to. Maybe it should look how God wanted it to look. Didn't God know best? Wasn't He really in control? If I believed that, why would I expect things to be the way I wanted them to be? If I believed God was in control and had brought me to these circumstances, or allowed them in my life, then maybe I needed to learn how to be content in every circumstance.

Look back on your own life. Think about the times when you matured the most and grew closer to God. Were they times of peace and calm water? Or were they during the storms in life, the tough times? I grew closer to God during the tough times; I was more dependent on Him then. During challenging times, nothing seemed to be working the way I wanted it to, so I had to decide whether I trusted God or my worldly wisdom. I knew I had to trust Him with all my heart.

Ultimately, I realized that the painting of the beautiful landscape was not how my life looked. From an earthly perspective, my life was not quiet, pretty, or filled with serenity. It seemed much more like the storm. Things outside of my control were always happening.

The storms in life always seem to be raging. We need to learn how to seek peace such as the mother bird found. This is God's peace, the peace that transcends all understanding. This peace comes when we have dependence on God and are confident that He is the one in control, not us. God has an eternal perspective for our lives that we cannot comprehend. We need to trust that He is leading us in the right direction, even when it seems things are messed up. We have to remember that we don't know it all; God does. Our trust is in Him, and that is where our peace comes from.

This story about the two paintings is significant to me because I was seeking the wrong peace; I was seeking something that was not possible, and I resented most everyone who got in the way of my achieving this picture of peace.

I don't want to confuse the issue here, but it is important that I tell you I do enjoy times when I am on vacation and my real life sometimes looks very similar to the landscape painting. But these times are almost artificial. I see them as mountaintop experiences God gives us to enjoy. Eventually, we have to come down and live in the valley the way it was designed. It is in the valley that life with Jesus is lived. This is where we learn from Him and grow. It is in the valley that the storm rages and we need to find His peace.

So how do you find peace when the storm of life is raging? What do you do when

- your daughter tells you she's pregnant by some guy she just met at a party?
- you lose your job and the bills continue to come crashing down?
- someone you love is diagnosed with terminal cancer?

- your spouse comes home drunk again?
- your spouse tells you he or she is having an affair?

When these kinds of circumstances entered my life, I tended to get shipwrecked. They significantly disturbed my picture of peace. I would say, "This was not part of my plan." But finally, I understood that I needed to seek the peace of God and let Him handle these circumstances.

I'm not advocating that we try to avoid our feelings when these things happen. I would probably have to be dead to not get somewhat upset if I lost my job. But after the emotions have run their course, we need to learn to handle them and then seek God's perfect peace. He is our true source of peace. So you may want to ask yourself, *When am I at peace?*

Let's consider something else. Do you sense that God is with you and that you are walking with Him? Do you go through your day seeing God, hearing from God, and experiencing Him? Paul eloquently wrote in the New Testament about following and living by the Spirit. Do you feel you are following and living by the Spirit? Let's look at Romans 8:12–14.

> Therefore, brothers and sisters, we have an obligation - but it is not to the flesh, to live according to it. For if you live according to the flesh, you will die; but if by the Spirit you put to death the misdeeds of the body, you will live. For those who are led by the Spirit of God are the children of God.

Notice Paul's use of the word *obligation*. He was saying that we have an obligation not to follow earthly wisdom or seek earthly material things, because we will die. Rather, we must follow the Holy Spirit, and we will live. If you are a child of God, then act like one by following the Holy Spirit. Do you follow the Holy Spirit? Are you doing what God asked you to do? When was the last time God gave you advice or told you to do something? Can you remember what it was? Did you do it? Do you regularly hear from God? Are you in conversation with Him as you go through your day? If you have a close relationship with Jesus, I believe you'll be in conversation with Him.

Do you find yourself setting your daily agenda and then asking God to bless it? Or do you pray and ask God for His guidance and then wait for His answer? Do you seek God's guidance in all your daily decisions, or just when you have a big decision to make?

If you have a close, personal, and intimate relationship with Jesus, the Holy Spirit will consume the old you from the inside. You will be a changed person, a new creation. You will have to talk about Jesus, so much so that if someone put duct tape over your mouth, the rocks next to you would start speaking on your behalf. You will want to, need to, and desire to be in His Word. You will want to pray and to serve others. These things will be as natural to you as breathing. Nobody will have to remind you to do them. You will just want to do them, and they will be done.

The thing to notice is not necessarily what you do, but why you do it. Is it out of duty that you do these things? Maybe you do them because you think they are good things to do. Maybe you do them because everyone around you will see you doing them, and that's important to you. But what if you do these things because this is who you are, God's creation with His Holy Spirit living inside you?

Maybe now you're saying, "Yes, I'd love to enjoy a close relationship with Jesus, but I have other things going on, and there's just no time. I have to work, clean the house, drive the kids, make dinner, mow the lawn, and paint the house. When I'm done with all these things, I'll need a break to watch my favorite TV show. And it's baseball season. You know I can't miss a game."

If this, or something close to it, is what you're thinking, then you might have to ask yourself some very hard questions. Is it possible you're not really following Jesus? Is it possible you've done the transaction, received the gift of the Holy Spirit, but buried the gift while waiting for the return of the master? Maybe you're slowly fading from Him and aren't even aware that you have a closer relationship with the world than you do with Jesus.

Maybe you feel that running your life without a close relationship with Jesus is okay because you've compared yourself to other Christians and come out looking pretty average. Their schedules and lifestyles look similar to yours; they're essentially doing the same things as you. How many times do we ask each other what we are doing and respond with something like, "I'm so busy." Have you ever wondered why you are so busy? Is your day filled with activities that you've decided to do, or with things you believe God has requested you to do? Maybe you're going to church and Bible study, helping people, and donating money, yet still, you know something's missing. Something in your heart tells you there must be more.

As you consider this, remember that when Jesus was with us about two thousand years ago, He invited many people to follow Him. He told them the cost of following Him was high. His invitation to potential followers was clearly more costly than the crowds were willing to accept. Many chose not to follow Him. Jesus was okay with that. He didn't beg or plead with them; He just spoke His truth and then moved on. Jesus knew that some would listen to His warning and change their behaviors, but others would think they knew better.

In his book *Radical*, David Platt wrote about our relationship with Jesus. Below, I have adapted a portion of the first chapter of his book.

This relationship with Jesus is a total, superior, exclusive devotion to Him. If you follow Jesus, you abandon everything. You abandon your needs. You abandon your personal desires. You abandon your possessions. Quite possibly, you even abandon your family and friends. We know that Jesus said all this in the Bible, but we don't want to believe it. We're afraid of what it might mean for our earthly lives. So we rationalize these passages away. Somehow, we come to the conclusion that Jesus didn't really mean this. In doing so, we keep redefining Christianity and create our own version of Jesus.

We are heading down a dangerous path when we convince ourselves that Jesus, our Lord and Savior, is something other than who He is. We are starting to turn Him into someone who isn't bothered by our materialism, wouldn't ask us to give away all we have, wouldn't expect us to turn away from a close relationship to be closer to Him, and is comfortable with our casual relationship and lukewarm devotion to

Him. We somehow believe He promised to materially bless us, bring us plush living quarters, fill our bank accounts, and allow us to live comfortable and prosperous lives. Thinking of Jesus like this starts to make Him look like what we want Him to look like. That is not how it's supposed to be. We are to be transformed to be more like Him.

I agree with what Mr. Platt wrote; we should be looking closely at our relationship with Jesus. Are we hoping He will conform to the wants we have for our lives, or will we choose to die to ourselves and then live for Him?

So, do you feel you're in a personal, intimate relationship with Jesus? Is your entire will and desire to live directed at following Him and His ways? Is God in your life much like a safety net for salvation, or does He have a significant impact on your day-to-day living?

From the standpoint of eternal life, does it matter? I know what's being taught in the church, but what does Jesus say?

Review Questions

- If we do all kinds of service work, does that mean we have a relationship with Jesus? Why or why not?
- Are there activities in your life that you place higher in importance than Jesus? What are they? Does it matter that they are more important to you than your relationship with Jesus is? Why or why not?
- Do you see yourself as someone who fits Jesus into their busy schedule, or as someone who is living a surrendered life and following Jesus? Please explain.

CHAPTER 11

Trust in Jesus

So, where do you go from here?

In this book, I have shown you many warnings that come right out of the Bible. Most of the warnings relate to our obedience and devotion to God, Jesus, and the Holy Spirit, but others relate to how we treat our earthly brothers and sisters. Do we love them? Do we put them before ourselves?

Many people don't want to hear warnings. Some say that I'm just scaring people into loving God, and that's wrong. Let's think about that perspective for a moment. As I mentioned earlier, those of us who are parents know that deep down, our children love structure. They might not say so and they might whine about the boundaries and structure we give them, but we give them structure, boundaries, and warnings for their own safety because we love them. We enforce the boundaries with real consequences; when our children cross them, they should expect the consequences we have told them about.

Do you think it is any different for God? Isn't He giving us boundaries and setting our expectations? Isn't He also telling us about the consequences of crossing these boundaries? Why do you think God does this? Because He's mean or wants us to be terrified of Him? No, God isn't mean, and He doesn't want us to be terrified of Him. Maybe you're thinking God wants to take the fun out of our lives. I don't believe this to be true either. I believe He is doing this because He loves us more than we can imagine. When we receive warnings and believe them to be credible, we have a responsibility to take them to heart and change what needs to changed.

Our only hope for salvation is through our dear Lord and Savior, Jesus Christ. Our relationship with Him is to be our number one priority. Jesus referred to Himself as the narrow gate, and He asked us to follow the narrow road. Look at what Jesus had to say about the small gate and narrow road in Matthew 7:13–14: "Enter through the narrow gate. For wide is the gate and broad is the road that leads to destruction, and many enter through it. But small is the gate and narrow the road that leads to life, and only a few find it."

In this verse, Jesus was explaining that He is the gate that leads to life. Many will not enter through the narrow gate and walk the narrow road, which leads to everlasting life. It is up to us to choose to do so. To walk the narrow road is to continuously repent of our sins, live our lives in complete surrender to Jesus, follow Him with all our might, and be in a deep, close, and intimate relationship with Him.

Doing this requires work, firm intentions, and effort. Sometimes, it requires pain and suffering. It's possible that walking this path may require us to live very different lives. On the other hand, it's possible that it will require very little change. There is only one way to find this out: by asking Him.

God created the path, Jesus is the gate leading to the path, and we all have the option, the free choice, to follow Jesus. If we choose not to follow and have a close relationship with Him, will we be denied entrance to heaven? Remember what happened to the foolish virgins who didn't live their lives in readiness: They were denied entrance into heaven. Jesus said He did not know them.

There are those who object to this and say, "Jesus came and died for us all. He took away the sins of the world. He paid the price so we wouldn't have to suffer the consequences of our sin." This is true, but does that mean that because Jesus died on the cross, everyone is going to heaven? No, not everyone is going to heaven.

So who does go to heaven? I know what's being taught in church, that those who do the transaction are going to heaven—but what did Jesus say? He actually had much to say about who goes to heaven, and none of it had anything to do with doing a transaction. It had everything to do with

- keeping our relationship with Him our top priority;
- following Him in all His ways;
- loving Him and others;
- serving Him and others;
- repenting and turning from our old, sinful desires; and
- living in the light of His grace, peace, and mercy.

I hope you take the time to pause now and consider how this applies to you. Think about the lifestyle Jesus is calling you to. Hopefully, He is calling you to a life devoted to following His ways. I believe Jesus sees the lifestyle choices we make and also knows the temptations before us. He wants us to be on guard as it relates to our walk with Him. I think He understands the distractions in our lives. Nonetheless, He holds us to some very high standards. He illustrated this with yet another parable in Luke 16:19–31.

> There was a rich man who was dressed in purple and fine linen and lived in luxury every day. At his gate was laid a beggar named Lazarus, covered with sores and longing to eat what fell from the rich man's table. Even the dogs came and licked his sores.
>
> The time came when the beggar died and the angels carried him to Abraham's side. The rich man also died and was buried. In hell, where he was in torment, he looked up and saw Abraham far away, with Lazarus by his side. So he called to him, "Father Abraham, have pity on me and send Lazarus to dip the tip of his finger in water and cool my tongue, because I am in agony in this fire."
>
> But Abraham replied, "Son, remember that in your lifetime you received your good things, while Lazarus received bad things, but now he is comforted here and you are in agony. And besides all this, between us

and you a great chasm has been fixed, so that those who want to go from here to you cannot, nor can anyone cross over from there to us."

He answered, "Then I beg you, father, send Lazarus to my father's house, for I have five brothers. Let him warn them, so that they will not also come to this place of torment." Abraham replied, "They have Moses and the Prophets; let them listen to them."

"No, father Abraham," he said, "but if someone from the dead goes to them, they will repent." He said to him, "If they do not listen to Moses and the Prophets, they will not be convinced even if someone rises from the dead."

What does Jesus want us to learn from this parable? Some people think this story demonstrates that if you're rich, you're going to hell. I don't think that was what Jesus was saying here. Clearly, the story is about a man of wealth and luxury who, in life, knew the poor Lazarus. You get the feeling that the rich man enjoyed his earthly high position; we know Lazarus longed to eat even a scrap from the rich man's table.

After they both died, the rich man sat in hell, in torment, and watched Lazarus enjoying life in heaven. The rich man received his happiness while on earth, and Lazarus got to enjoy eternity with Jesus in heaven.

The part of the parable that I want to bring to your attention is at the end, when the rich man asked Abraham to send Lazarus to warn his family so they wouldn't have to live in torment in hell. The rich man said his brothers would listen to a dead man's warning. But Jesus said, "If they do not listen to Moses and the Prophets, they will not be convinced even if someone rises from the dead."

Can't you just hear Jesus asking, "What will it take for people to believe in me and follow me? They've seen the miracles, they've seen me face to face, they've seen my Father in heaven raise me from the dead, but they still won't believe. Some people you can warn, but they just won't listen. They're stiff-necked and live life on their own terms." Hearing the warnings of Jesus and not paying attention to them—now that's risky behavior.

Think about your situation. Could the message you're receiving as you read what Jesus said in the Bible be a warning to you? If so, are you living like the rich man, not too concerned about your eternal life with Jesus? After all, you've done the transaction and are going to heaven. Right?

Well, what if they are wrong? What if your entrance into heaven is yet to be decided, just as Jesus said and as you have been reading? Who are you going to believe? Jesus or anyone else? I hope you'll believe Jesus. You've been reading His words. If you believe what Jesus said, will your behavior change? Do you think the rich man in the parable wished he could have gone back and had a do-over?

Consider once again what Jesus said when He spoke about being the small gate and narrow path we can choose to walk. It sounds like a rather stern warning to me. Is that warning applicable to you? Are you walking the broad

road or the narrow path? Why did Jesus say that only a few would find it? Do you think He knows that many people will hear His Word in the Bible, but not follow Him? Many people heard Jesus speak over two thousand years ago, yet they chose not to follow Him. The teaching was hard; the standard was high.

Some people tell me that our eternal life is not everything and that we can and should enjoy a little "heaven on earth." I agree with this statement somewhat, but it's sometimes taken out of context. There's nothing wrong with enjoying a little heaven on earth, but maybe we're enjoying things in ways that are more than just a little heaven on earth. Maybe we are enjoying our materialism, our vacations, our leisure, and our sports too much. Maybe in some weird way, we enjoy life on our own terms too much. Sometimes, these things can cause us to walk apart from Jesus. Well, Jesus had something to say about this. Let's review another verse in Matthew.

Earlier in this book, we went over Matthew 5:29–30, a very similar verse to this one. The gospel writers were not often repetitive; when they were, it was to give their statements more emphasis. I think Matthew wanted to make sure we understood this principle in Matthew 18:8–9.

> If your hand or your foot causes you to sin, cut it off and throw it away. It is better for you to enter life maimed or crippled than to have two hands or two feet and be thrown into eternal fire. And if your eye causes you to sin, gouge it out and throw it away. It is better for you to enter life with one eye

than to have two eyes and be thrown in to
the fire of hell.

Jesus was not actually saying that everyone must cut off a hand or foot or gouge out an eye; He was saying that if something was causing us to sin (or lose focus on Him), then it was better to get rid of it. Jesus knew how important our hands, feet, and eyes are to us, yet He said that whatever causes us to sin in our walk with Him, we are better off getting rid of it—even if it is a hand, foot, or eye.

I hope that you deeply consider what we call a little heaven on earth and focus on what Jesus is calling us to. He wants us to follow Him in all our ways and to have a deep, close, and intimate relationship with Him. I believe Jesus means what He says. I hope you do too!

Is it possible that you may be denied entrance to heaven if you're not trying to follow Jesus with all your heart, mind, body, and soul? When you die your earthly death, you will have your own meeting with Jesus. During this time, He will determine whether you will live for eternity in heaven or in hell. Think about what He will ask you. What will be the basis of His judgment? Do you believe He will ask only whether you did the transaction, and that will decide the matter? Or do you think He will ask some additional questions when He judges where you will spend your eternal life?

Will He ask if you followed him? If He does, what will you say?

Will He be able to say that you were born again?

Will He say that He knows you?

Will He say, "Well done, faithful servant"?

Will He say He has a close, personal, and intimate relationship with you?

Will He say your faith is like that of a child?

Will He say that you blended in with the crowd of nonbelievers, or that you stood out?

Will He say that you lived your life like you believed?

Will Jesus ask you about your material possessions? Are you a rich young person with your earthly possessions separating you from a relationship with Jesus?

Will Jesus say that you built your home on the foundation of your faith in Him?

Will Jesus say you were willing to pay the price to follow Him?

Will Jesus say you gave it your everything?

Will Jesus say that your righteousness surpassed that of the Pharisees?

Will Jesus say you remained angry with a brother or sister?

Will Jesus say you pursued the kingdom of God as if it were a hidden treasure?

Will Jesus say you loved God with all your heart, mind, body, and soul?

Will Jesus say you loved your neighbor as yourself?

What will you tell Jesus when He asks if you were like the faithful servant, who continued to do His work while He was away?

Will Jesus say you stood firm to the end?

Will Jesus say you cared for the poor?

Will Jesus say you put your hand to the plow and did not look back?

Will Jesus say you cared for the hungry?

Will Jesus say you lived in readiness for His return?

Will Jesus say you put His gifts and talents to use to further His kingdom?

How will you respond when He talks to you about the vine and the branches and asks you if you remained in Him?

Will He say you came to the banquet when you were invited?

Will Jesus see you as someone in the stadium stands or someone on the field?

Will Jesus tell you to go to heaven or hell?

Many churches teach that if you have done the transaction, Jesus will welcome you into heaven, regardless of how you lived your life after that point. What did Jesus have to say about this? What do you think? Think carefully about this: What if they are wrong? What if your eternal life is also dependent on the quality of your relationship with Jesus? Who are you going to believe?

I say, put your trust in Jesus and what He says in His living Word, the Holy Bible.

Amen!

AFTERWORD

Thank you for reading the message God has for you in this book. He is the Creator of all things, including this book. I pray His love grows in your heart.

If you want to talk more about the topics in this book, I would enjoy hearing from you. At my website, www. theysayyouaresaved.com, you will find several ways to get in touch with me. You can also send me an e-mail at theysayyouaresaved@comcast.net.

If you are considering doing a more in-depth study of the topics in this book, please send me an email and I will send you a 10 week course outline that I have developed.

If you are part of a group that would like me to come and speak about this topic, please do let me know; I will do what I can to accommodate your requests.

A SHORT BIBLE STUDY

I developed this short Bible study to get us grounded in some truth relating to the topic of salvation and the end times as spoken about by Jesus. I thought that might be best accomplished by doing a short study that involves reading two chapters from the Bible, Matthew 24 and 25.

Please take your time with this study. Pray before you read these two chapters, and ask the Holy Spirit to give you His divine interpretation.

These chapters will be discussed in detail in this book. Please don't look ahead; just read the Bible, ask the Spirit to guide you, and write down your answers to the questions. (You may want to consider reviewing your answers with other Christians.)

Who was Jesus addressing in these two chapters?

What was He trying to explain?

In Matthew 24:1–3, what questions did the disciples ask Jesus?

What warning did Jesus give His disciples in Matthew 24:4–14?

What does verse 10 mean to you?

According to verse 13, who will be saved?

How did Jesus describe the end of the age in Matthew 24:15–35?

According to Jesus in Matthew 24:36–44, who knows when the end times will be?

In verse 37, what did Jesus compare the end of time to?

Before the flood, what were the people doing?

What happened to them?

Was there something else they should have been doing that might have yielded a different result?

Does Jesus's comparison of Noah and the end of the age apply to you and your life? How?

In Matthew 24:45–51, Jesus gave us an example of a wise servant. Who is the master?

Who is the servant?

What was the servant responsible for?

What happened to the servant when the master returned and he was doing what he was responsible for?

What happened to the servant when the master returned and he was not doing what he was supposed to?

Is this parable applicable to you? How?

Will it matter we are not doing what we are supposed to be doing when Jesus returns? If so, how will it matter?

Have you ever wondered what we are supposed to be doing while Jesus is away? Explain.

Parable of the ten virgins - Matthew 25:1-13

Who do the virgins represent in the parable contained in Matthew 25:1–13?

Describe the difference between the wise and the foolish virgins.

Who is the bridegroom?

When the bridegroom comes, what did they hear?

Then what were the virgins trying to do?

The wise virgins were able to do what?

What did the foolish virgins have to do?

Why did the foolish virgins have to do this?

What happened to the wise virgins?

While the foolish virgins were purchasing oil, what happened?

When the foolish virgins knocked on the door to heaven, what did Jesus tell them?

In verse 13, Jesus says to keep watch. What does that mean?

Is this parable applicable to you? How?

Does it matter if we are not keeping watch for when Jesus returns? If so, what does it matter?

Parable of the bags of gold - Matthew 25:14–30

In the parable of the bags of gold, who is the man going on the journey?

Who are the servants in the parable?

What do you think the talents represent?

How long was the man gone?

What did the servant with five talents do with them?

What did he receive?

What did the servant with two talents do with them?

What did he receive?

What did the servant with one talent do with it?

What did he receive?

Describe what a person today would be doing that would be similar to burying a talent given him.

Jesus said in verse 30 that the servant who was given one talent was "thrown outside into the darkness, where there will be weeping and gnashing of teeth." Where do you think this is?

Does this parable apply to you? How?

Are you putting the talent Jesus gave you to work?

Does it matter if we are not putting our talents to work? If so, what does it matter?

Parable of the Sheep and the Goats – Matthew 25:31-46

In the parable, who is the Son of Man?

According to what Jesus said in verse 32, what will the Son of Man do?

The sheep will be on the right of the Son of Man. According to what Jesus said in verse 34, what will they receive?

According to verses 35–36, what did the sheep do?

According to verses 37–39, did those considered sheep actually see the Son of Man and serve Him? Whom did they serve?

The goats will be on the left of the Son of Man. According to what Jesus said in verse 41, what will they receive?

According to verses 41–43, what did the goats not do?

According to verses 44–45, did the goats see the Son of Man and not serve Him? Whom did they not serve?

According to verse 46, where will the sheep go? Where will the goats go?

Does this parable apply to you? How?

Please consider the following questions.

- Are you feeding the hungry of the world?
- Are you quenching the thirst of those without water?
- Are you open and generous to strangers?
- Do you clothe those who have no clothes?
- Do you care for the sick?
- Do you visit those in prison?

When the Son of Man returns, how will you be able to answer these questions?

Do you think the Son of Man will consider you a goat or a sheep?

Does it matter?

I congratulate you on completing this short Bible study. There were many deep and thought-provoking questions that you had to consider.

The question, "Does it matter?" will be discussed throughout this book. Please consider what the Spirit is telling you as you ponder this question and read this book.

REFERENCES

Chambers, Oswald. *My Utmost For His Highest*. Uhrichsville: Discovery House, 1992.

Platt, David. *Radical*. Colorado Springs: Multnomah Books, 2010.

SCRIPTURE REFERENCES

I created this section to locate the many bible verses used within this book. I used a paraphrase or an abbreviation of the verse to help identify it. Please refer to your bible or the referenced page in the book for the complete verse and context.

Exodus
20:20 – fear of God, keep from sinning – p9

Numbers
14:11-12 – how long, refuse to believe in me – p18

Deuteronomy
5:29 – fear me, might go well with them – p10
10:12 – fear the Lord your God – p8

Psalms
33:18 – eyes of the Lord, on those who fear him – p9
78:32-37 – in spite of his wonders, they did not believe – p16
139:23 – search me oh God and know my heart – p96

Proverbs
1:7 – fear of the Lord, beginning of knowledge – p8

Ecclesiastes
12:13 – fear God and keep His commandments – p9

Matthew
5:20 – righteousness surpass that of the Pharisees – p39
5:22 – says 'you fool', danger of the fire of hell – p40
5:29-30 – lose one part of body, not whole body into hell – p37
7:13-14 – the narrow and wide gate – p107
7:21-23 – not everyone who says 'Lord' will enter kingdom of heaven – p50
7:24-27 – wise and foolish builders – p50
13:44-46 – parables, the hidden treasure and the pearl – p58
18:3-5 – unless you change, little children, never enter kingdom of heaven – p40
18:8-9 – better to live maimed than have hands, feet, but into eternal fire – p113
19:16-30 – rich man, hard for the rich to enter kingdom of heaven – p31
Ch 24-25 – end of times, parables of the virgins, talents, sheep and goats – p63

Mark
10:14-15 – anyone not receive kingdom of God like child will never enter it – p41
13:12-13 – one who stands firm to the end will be saved – p42

16:15-18 – these signs will accompany those who
believe – p14

Luke
9:57-62 – foxes have dens, birds have nests – p35
10:24-37 – The parable of the good Samaritan – p58
12:42-46 – good for servant to be doing what the master
asked – p41
13:24-30 – we ate and drank with you. 'I don't know
you' – p51
14:16-24 – parable of the great banquet – p53
14:25-35 – those who do not give up everything, cannot
be my disciple – p42
16:19-31 – The rich man and Lazarus – p109

John
3:3 – cannot see the kingdom of God unless born
again – p44
3:16 – For God so loved the world – p12
5:20-24 – father judges no one, entrusted all judgment to
the Son – p29
5:26-29 – those who have done what is good will rise to
live – p30
5:39-44 – how can you believe since you accept glory
from one another – p54
6:47-58 – I am the bread of life, eat my flesh, drink my
blood – p55
15:6 – if you do not remain in me, like a branch, thrown
into the fire – p28 & p86
16:33 – in this world you will have trouble – p89

Acts
9:31 – living in the fear of the Lord, encouraged by the Holy Spirit – p9

Romans
8:12-14 – if you live according to the flesh you will die – p1 & p101

Galatians
1:2 – to the churches in Galatia – p29
5:19-20 – those who live like this will not inherit the kingdom of God – p28

Ephesians
2:8-9 – for it is by grace you have been saved, through faith – p23

Colossians
3:5-10 – put to death, whatever belong so your earthly nature – p57

1 Thessalonians
5:16-18 – rejoice always, pray continuously, thanks in all circumstances – p96

James
2:14-19 – faith, not accompanied by action, is dead – p88

Revelation
14:7 – fear God and give him glory, worship him who made the heavens – p8

Printed in the United States
By Bookmasters